THE NEW STAR CHAMBER AND OTHER ESSAYS
Annotated Edition

THE NEW STAR CHAMBER
AND OTHER ESSAYS

Annotated Edition

EDGAR LEE MASTERS

Edited by Jason Stacy

Associate Editors: Brandon Adams, Scott Both, Joseph Davis, Shawn Emily, Jessica Guldner, Amy Kapp, Joseph King, Andrew Niederhauser, Abbigayle Schaefer, Elizabeth Schroader, Andrew Shepard, Nicholas Swain, and Lucas Turnbull

Southern Illinois University Press / *Carbondale and Edwardsville*

Southern Illinois University Press
www.siupress.com

26 25 24 23   4 3 2 1

Publication of this volume has been made possible in part through the support
of Herbert K. and Thyra Russell and the SIUE College of Arts and Sciences,
History Department.

Cover illustration by Hannah Holste and text illustrations by Adrian Hanzel

Library of Congress Cataloging-in-Publication Data

Names: Masters, Edgar Lee, 1868– author. | Stacy, Jason, 1970– editor.
Title: The new star chamber and other essays / Edgar Lee Masters ; edited by
    Jason Stacy . . . [and thirteen others].
Description: Annotated edition. | Carbondale : Southern Illinois University
    Press, 2023. | Includes bibliographical references. | Summary: "Edited and
    produced by university students, The New Star Chamber and Other Essays
    offers a compelling critique of corporate capitalism and American imperialism.
    In print again for the first time since 1904, this edition includes an introduction
    and historical annotations throughout"—Provided by publisher.
Identifiers: LCCN 2022049887 (print) | LCCN 2022049888 (ebook) |
    ISBN 9780809370108 (paperback) | ISBN 9780809370115 (ebook)
Subjects: LCSH: Masters, Edgar Lee, 1868—Political and social views.
    | United States—Colonial question. | United States—Politics and
    government—1901–1909. | Statesmen—United States. | Imperialism—
    United States. | Capitalism—United States.
Classification: LCC E173 .M42 2023 (print) | LCC E173 (ebook) |
    DDC 973—dc23/eng/20221229
LC record available at https://lccn.loc.gov/2022049887
LC ebook record available at https://lccn.loc.gov/2022049888

Printed on recycled paper ♻

SIU
Southern Illinois University System

Contents

Editors' Foreword
Notes on the Text

"An historical methods seminar that required completion of a group of edited documents . . . would produce better historians and better editors."
—Charles T. Cullen

Students at Southern Illinois University Edwardsville introduced and annotated this edition of *The New Star Chamber and Other Essays* in a course taught by Jason Stacy called Editing History (HIST 446). Students at Southern Illinois University Carbondale designed and produced this edition in courses called Typography I (AD 222) and Graphic Design II (AD 452), both taught by Corey Tester, and Communication Drawing (AD 122), taught by Jason Wonnell.

Many of the essays here first appeared in the *Chicago Chronicle* in 1900 and 1901. The Hammersmark Publishing Company of Chicago published them, along with new pieces, as *The New Star Chamber and Other Essays* in 1904.

In this edition, we have sought a balance between fidelity to the 1904 edition with readability. Throughout, we note as necessary variant spellings of common words and silently revise likely compositor errors of punctuation, spelling, and capitalization.

Acknowledgments

This project was supported by Herbert K. Russell, whose *Edgar Lee Masters: A Biography* proved to be an invaluable resource. We are also grateful for SIUE's Department of History and for Southern Illinois University Press, especially Jennifer Egan and Amy Etcheson, who saw promise in the project. Thanks, also, to Jessica Guldner for assistance in building the index and reviewing the proofs.

And to our families and friends: you make all our work possible.

THE NEW STAR CHAMBER AND OTHER ESSAYS

Annotated Edition

INTRODUCTION

EDGAR Lee Masters published *The New Star Chamber and Other Essays* in 1904 in Chicago. Born in Garnett, Kansas, on August 23, 1868, to Hardin and Emma Masters (née Dexter), Masters lived in Petersburg, Illinois, until he was eleven years old and then moved to nearby Lewistown, where he lived until 1892, with a short sojourn at Galesburg's Knox Academy, a preparatory school affiliated with Knox College. The Spoon River, near Lewistown, inspired Masters to publish his most notable work, *Spoon River Anthology*, in 1915, a collection of fictional epitaphs by the dead in a small-town cemetery.

From a young age, Masters's expectations for his own life differed from the expectations of those around him. His grandfather, Squire Davis Masters, wanted him to pursue a career in farming, and through Squire Davis, Masters developed a romanticized ideal of the American farmer, an attitude that he carried throughout his life. His father, Hardin, wanted him to pursue law.[1] Masters, though, wished to become a writer.[2] These opposing forces manifested themselves throughout Masters's life as he proved unable to commit to one career. These countervailing motivations also bled into the pages of *The New Star Chamber*.

Masters became a lawyer in 1891 and moved to Chicago in 1892 where he was exposed to many new social and political trends. He described his early years in Chicago as a period of introspection that brought him "face to face with people" and introduced him to a "life of action."[3] Through his sister's marriage into wealth in 1893[4] and his own marriage to the daughter of a successful businessman five years later, Masters was inducted into high society, though he proved ambivalent to its trappings. During this same period, in 1896, Masters jumped into the presidential campaign of Democratic nominee William Jennings Bryan. Masters perceived Bryan and his Populist-infused Democratic platform as the beginning of a "changed America."[5] Masters supported Bryan on issues such as the increase of silver coinage, which he believed would alleviate the debt of the working farmer. In 1898, when the United States declared war on Spain, Masters, along with other prominent Populists like Bryan and contemporaneous Progressives like Jane Addams, saw the war as an imperialist adventure, contrary to the traditional ideals of the United States. To Masters, American imperialism proved fatal to the Jeffersonian ideal of a peaceful, agrarian republic, a kind of national version of the nostalgia he felt for his grandfather's farm.[6] In 1903, Masters and Clarence Darrow, whose labor activism overlapped with some of Masters's own political views on labor, became law partners.[7]

Nineteenth-century discourses around masculinity also shaped Masters during this period. The gender historian E. Anthony Rotundo argues that there were three archetypes of an ideal man in the nineteenth century: the masculine achiever, the Christian gentleman, and the masculine primitive.[8] Looking at the male relatives in Edgar Lee Masters's life through this perspective, we can categorize them according to these archetypes. Squire Davis, whom Masters idealized, fell into the second archetype, a Christian gentleman farmer, representative of a distant, better time. While Masters rejected his grandfather's religiosity, he did so primarily for the hypocrisy he perceived it bred in others. Squire Davis's faith and practice remained unsullied in Masters's mind, though it represented an American Elysium that could never be regained. Squire Davis did not drink and was full of compassion, love, and kindness, according to his grandson. Masters's father, Hardin, exemplified the masculine primitive for his son. Edgar Lee saw in Hardin's love of male camaraderie, drinking, and loose marital fidelity a kind of *joie de vivre*. Masters himself shaped his life around the archetype of the masculine achiever, which pitted itself against other men in the rough-and-tumble world of the modern industrial economy. In this light, Masters's repeated infidelities, occasional drinking, and roving pursuit of self-actualization matched his father's lifestyle, though his professional waywardness marked him as an ambivalent careerist who struggled to define himself professionally. In effect, Hardin proved to be an influence on how Masters acted, while Squire Davis influenced his ideals. This made Masters a kind of fallen version of his grandfather's type and a more unhappily professional version of his father.

Location further shaped Masters's development of masculinity. By the mid-nineteenth century, the city, a place of competition, and the country, a place of repose, offered a simple dichotomy for two types of masculine lifestyle. According to Michael S. Kimmel, "American men chose both."[9] Thus, despite the fact that he moved to Chicago in 1892, he cultivated a small farm in Michigan later in life, perhaps drawing on his simplified memories of his hometowns of Lewistown and Petersburg.[10] In this light, *Spoon River Anthology* reads like a drama of rural life where human dilemmas prove eternal. On the other hand, the essays in *The New Star Chamber*, published eleven years before, are passionate arguments about current issues; they are Masters inserting himself into up-to-the-minute events. It is also important to recall that these essays were published at the height of Masters's legal career, exemplifying all the facts and dramatic pathos necessary for courtroom drama.

But Masters's writing interests were, at heart, literary. After *Spoon River Anthology* was published to acclaim in 1915, he continued to publish works of literature, though none reached its level of success. This work continued to reflect his nostalgia for a lost America, with perhaps the most notable being *Lincoln: The Man* in 1931, a book so polarizing in its critique of the sixteenth president that Masters received hate mail, mutilated pictures of himself, and an endorsement from the Sons of Confederate Veterans.[11]

Masters died in 1950 in Pennsylvania, having quit the law, divorced his wife, remarried, and attempted to make a life of writing. These choices tracked the conflicting ideologies and experiences of the man: an urban lawyer whose most famous book focused on rural life, an advocate for the downtrodden who blamed Abraham Lincoln for modern injustice, and an anti-imperialist who celebrated America's pioneering past. Reflective of his time while ever at odds with it, Edgar Lee Masters attempted to craft a writing life to shape his ever-changing world. *The New Star Chamber* is an exemplary source for understanding this complicated author in the midst of his transformation from urban lawyer to poet of rural America.

PART-TIME POPULIST

Although Edgar Lee Masters often wrote about subjects that reflected admiration for the Populist Party of the late nineteenth and early twentieth centuries, he was not a typical Populist. And while the height of the movement coincided with Masters's young adulthood in the 1890s, he was too young to experience the party's origins. Masters admired the party's farmer-activists and their legacy yet never had any real experience with the struggles of agriculturalists during his childhood. He played little to no role in the rise of Populism as a political force.

"Populism" is a contested term among American historians. Beginning in the 1930s the movement was praised by historians for its advocacy of the rural farmer and industrial worker against businesses and banking interests during the Gilded Age.[12] Masters himself, as a Chicago lawyer, reflected these positions as he fought for members of the working class in many of his cases.[13] By the 1950s, historians increasingly viewed the party's activism as unrealistic, a kind of paranoid last gasp of rural America,[14] and attributed the rise of the movement to an increasingly cosmopolitan culture and economy that threatened the values of rural America. Masters saw this threat and often praised the past; he had few positive visions of the future. More recently, historians of Populism have illuminated its more progressive attributes, specifically the movement's sense that economic justice and social reform went hand in hand with industrial efficiency and government activism.[15] Today, however, populism, as a more general term, is often associated with the nostalgic political Right, adhering to the goal of making the nation great "again." Elements of *The New Star Chamber* fit this mood as well.

To better understand Masters's support of the Populist movement, it is important to recognize the political climate at the height of Populism in the 1890s. After the Civil War, farmers moving west of the Mississippi River chased land guaranteed by the Homestead Act (1862) and opportunities offered by expanding railroads. These new "Middle West" homesteaders strived to achieve their own iteration of the American dream by establishing thriving farms and agricultural communities. Squire Davis Masters purchased his own farm located north of Petersburg in the 1840s and built it into an orderly and successful homestead, which Masters visited throughout his childhood and idolized as an adult.[16] However, Masters's grandfather experienced little of the economic hardship faced by agriculturalists after the Civil War. During the 1880s, as newly settled farmers produced staple crops like corn and wheat at unprecedented rates, and as transportation costs fell with the expansion of railroads, crop prices dropped while farmer indebtedness remained stable. Prominent on the list of Populist reforms was the improvement of educational resources, scientific and technological advancements, support for labor rights, control of corporations, and the advocacy of silver as a valid currency to alleviate indebtedness. By 1890, the Populists exerted increasing pressure on the Democratic Party, and William Jennings Bryan, a Nebraska lawyer, Democrat, and popular orator, ran for a seat in the House of Representatives by advocating for the expansion of silver currency, a reflection of rising Populist sentiment among Democrats. His talent for public speaking was a driving force behind his success in the 1890 congressional campaign, winning him a seat in the House. The People's Party formed in 1892 and ran a strong third-party campaign with former Civil War general James B. Weaver at the top of the ticket. In the 1896 presidential election, Bryan ran for the presidency on both the Democratic and People's Party tickets.[17] This is the campaign that exposed Edgar Lee Masters to Bryan's speeches and Populist ideology, earning Bryan a place in Masters's mind as the ideal politician through whom to rescue the nation from rapacious industrial capitalism.

But Masters, while supporting Populist policies and a romantic ideal of the American farmer, was not quite a Populist himself. His political upbringing had been shaped by Jacksonian Democrats back to his grandfather's generation. Both Hardin and Squire Davis Masters were ambivalent towards Lincoln's policies during the Civil War. After the war, Hardin struggled to build his law career for a short time, having been labeled a "Copperhead" for his support of Democrats who rejected Lincoln's policies.[18] Nevertheless, by the 1890s, Hardin's connections to the Democratic Party in Illinois allowed him access to the 1896 Democratic National Convention in Chicago, where Bryan delivered his famous "Cross of Gold" speech. Hardin brought his son to the convention at a time when Edgar Lee was just starting his own legal career in the city. At the convention, Edgar Lee and Hardin heard speeches from John Peter Altgeld, the twentieth governor of Illinois, and David B. Hill, senator from New York, among others.[19] Masters was most moved by Bryan, as was his father, and both were convinced that "Andrew Jackson had come back in the person of Bryan" to "reclaim the country from the banks and syndicates who had robbed the people since 1861."[20]

While Masters admired Bryan and shared a nostalgic vision of the American farmer with other Populists, his inclinations kept him firmly within the Democratic Party, especially the wing that proved ambivalent toward the industrial capitalism of the era. In this regard, Governor Altgeld, as much as Bryan, influenced Masters's politics, not as a Populist but as a reform Democrat. Altgeld was a leading Democrat who supported labor, as seen by his advocacy for the Pullman strikers in 1894 and his pardoning of three activists convicted in the aftermath of the 1886 Haymarket Affair. Likewise, Bryan achieved the nomination for the Populist ticket in 1896 only after he was nominated by the Democrats for his insurgent support of silver currency. Bryan remained a Democrat for the rest of his political career. Edgar Lee Masters did too.

Although Masters was not really a Populist Party activist, it might be easy to confuse him with one, especially after reading his hagiography of Bryan in *The New Star Chamber*. However, Masters's admiration of Bryan reflects a Democrat's partisanship rather than a Populist's. Bryan ran unsuccessfully twice more for the presidency after 1896, in 1900 and 1908. In both cases, he ran solely on the Democratic ticket. By that time, the Populist Party had largely disappeared.

(IM)PERFECT PROGRESSIVE

The publication date of *The New Star Chamber*, 1904, places Masters's work at the temporal boundary between the demise of the Populist movement and the rise of national Progressivism. Masters never fully embraced either, picking and choosing aspects that appealed to a man of his upbringing and station. While fully supporting the anti–big business rhetoric espoused by the Progressives, Masters proved consistently ambivalent about the middle-class idealism characteristic of the era.[21] A patron of prostitutes in his young adulthood and an unfaithful husband later, Masters spared few words in the polemical *New Star Chamber* for women, the family, or the burgeoning suffrage movement, concentrating instead on the risks to democracy posed by the government, its agents, and its history. Ultimately, Masters's politics fell on the side it was always on: his own.

Rapid industrialization in the late nineteenth and early twentieth centuries and its negative effects were some of the main driving forces behind the Progressive movement's attempts at reform. Corporations made good use of the transition from rural to urban life in the big cities. The lure of wage work, disposable income, and the new leisure activities of a burgeoning consumer culture led to unchecked urban growth. Political corruption across all levels of government, coupled with the lack of social, cultural, and technological infrastructure and support services, created a heterogeneous urban environment rife with desperation and desolation.

The social reformers of the Progressive movement wanted to make changes to the unsafe urban environment, which included long working hours, minimal safety standards, and repetitive and solitary jobs that prized efficiency and productivity over humanity. Such attempts were often stymied by the corruption of the court system, which served factory owners at the expense of the working class, as industrial wealth made bribery common and legal protection of corporate monopolistic practices virtually unassailable.[22] According to Michael McGerr, "Bigness, interdependence, limits—these realities compelled Americans to reconsider the right of businesses, large and small, to do as they pleased."[23]

Masters, holding a romanticized view of antebellum American society due in part to his gentleman-farmer grandfather's influence, abhorred the social changes wrought by the American industrial economy in the aftermath of the Civil War. Placing the blame squarely upon the unchecked capitalism of leading elites and industrialists, Masters traced the roots of this corruption to the very origins of the American republic, enshrined within the Constitution, which fostered conditions that paved the way for the expansion of federal power and industrialization after the Civil War.[24] To Masters, this nefarious perversion of democracy was rooted in the tyranny of the Republican Party, an inheritor of the anti-democratic ideology of eighteenth-century ideologues like Alexander Hamilton and nineteenth-century legal theorists like Chief Justice John Marshall who fostered an elite stranglehold on federal power.[25]

Tinged with "Lost Cause" rhetoric rooted in his father's affinity for the Confederacy, *The New Star Chamber* reads like a retrospective melodrama of heroes and villains. Therefore, at first blush, these essays appear to personify the tone of the Progressive movement, which often also deployed heated rhetoric for the sake of reform.[26] However, upon careful reading, Masters's retrograde vision of an ideal nation comes to the fore. While for the Progressives, reform lay in the future, for Masters, a better nation lay in the past.

Conspicuously absent from Masters's political reverie is any mention of one of the defining features of the Progressive movement: the growing American middle class. The transition from Populism to Progressivism was marked by the assumption of the mantle of reform by a bourgeoisie anxious to contain an increasingly heterogeneous society riven by class, racial, and gender conflict. That Masters completely ignored these developments speaks to his antipathy toward the social aspects of the political movements he straddled. As McGerr points out, the Progressive movement emerged from a middle class uncomfortable with its own wealth and greatly disturbed by the consumerism and morality of the upper and lower classes surrounding it.[27] Temperance and moderation in all respects proved to be the remedy for these reformers, necessitating a program of moral and cultural uplift that sought to remake all Americans in the middle-class mold. This program of transformation began in the home, requiring the renegotiation of norms of behavior so that the nation could be revitalized from the parlor. Reining in prostitution and alcohol consumption and providing women with the franchise were the first steps toward a more equitable balance within the home, along with an attendant easing of domestic burdens and increased public opportunities for women. The education of children and their removal from the workforce were secondary goals to this reimagined cult of domesticity.[28]

Masters offers no words for or against these reforms in *The New Star Chamber*, ignoring them in favor of a narrow set of bugaboos: imperialism, corporations, and an overweening federal government. So concerned was Masters with the current political climate and insidious bogeymen, both historical and contemporaneous, that no mention is made of the family, marriage, women, child labor, racial oppression, or even, in specific terms, the rights of labor. It is as if these issues of significance to the reform impulse of his era were immaterial to Masters.

However, once we take Masters's own personal history into account, the reason for these omissions becomes obvious. Known for his inability to remain faithful to his wives or string of mistresses, Masters frequented brothels, was a drinker, and smoker. Finding little comfort in the trappings of hearth and home, Masters was unwilling to espouse the virtues of marriage and children. His parents' unhappy marriage provided his primary example of domestic "bliss," and Masters went on to emulate his father's womanizing and lifestyle explicitly.[29]

But in some realms, the reform ideals of Masters and the Progressives converged. One of the greatest victories the Progressives achieved was the direct election of U.S. senators with the ratification of the Seventeenth Amendment to the Constitution, a position previously endorsed by the People's Party in the Omaha Platform of 1892.[30] Prior to 1913, U.S. senators were elected by the legislatures of each state. Many Progressives viewed this as an unfair system, which promoted the long careers of state legislators who benefited from the various political machines developing across the nation. Throughout his essays in *The New Star Chamber*, Masters consistently argues that the rights and liberties of citizens were being infringed upon by the gulf between the electorate and its representatives. The essays "The New Star Chamber" and "Elect the Federal Judges" similarly express the danger of a monopolization of power in the federal courts. Masters's wish to reform the federal court system through election echoed a core belief of the Progressive movement: democratic practice promoted social justice, thereby marking one of the areas of convergence between Progressives and Masters.

Should Masters be considered a Progressive? Though he espoused views that fell within Progressive ideology, especially an antipathy toward corrupt government and overly powerful corporations, Masters's nostalgic vision of Jeffersonian states' rights and individualism ultimately place him outside mainstream Progressive policy. In the end, Masters cannot be reconciled to any vital political philosophy of his time. As an urban Populist who came late to the movement, Masters's bourgeois milieu proved socially more conducive to Progressivism, but his Manichaean interpretation of early American history and nostalgia for an antebellum agrarian republic placed him at odds with much of the reform atmosphere of his time. In this regard, Masters's eclecticism makes him a difficult figure to pigeonhole ideologically.

POSEUR PIONEER AND ANTI-IMPERIALIST

A recurring refrain championed by many, but not all, Populists and Progressives was a resistance to imperialist expansion, a stance that Masters embraced. However, a seeming dilemma lies at the core of Masters's anti-imperialist rhetoric: How could an anti-imperialist so fervently celebrate the nation's pioneering past, with all its attendant conquest and destruction of Native peoples?

For Masters, Presidents William McKinley and Theodore Roosevelt represented a departure from the ideals established by the Declaration of Independence, where governments were founded upon the consent of the governed. For an avowed Jeffersonian like Masters, McKinley and Roosevelt epitomized the culmination of two generations of Republican assault on proper democratic practice through the elevation of corporate interests; behind these changes lay the legacy of Alexander Hamilton and his elite inclinations. According to Masters, American entry into the Spanish-American War (1898) and the anti-Filipino counterinsurgency thereafter marked the exportation of industrial domination from the American continent to the rest of the world. Roosevelt proved the more strong-willed, opinionated, ambitious, and therefore dangerous leader. Comparing Masters's essays on Hamilton and Roosevelt in *The New Star Chamber* reveals that Masters believed Roosevelt manifested Hamilton's anti-democratic spirit, one that sought to expand American empire in order to benefit domestic elites, the president's claims to uplift colonized people notwithstanding. Exemplifying this paternalism, Roosevelt framed the occupation of the Philippines as doubly beneficial by providing an abundance of resources for the United States while providing a civilizing influence on the Filipino people until they could "stand alone."[31] By mouthing benevolence while practicing exploitation, American corporations, and their political handmaidens like Roosevelt, were able, according to Masters, to expand the oppression they had already inflicted upon American citizens.

Masters was not alone in his anti-imperialist inclinations. Across the political spectrum, anti-imperialists opposed American overseas expansion for diverse reasons.[32] Massachusetts Republican George Frisbie Hoar argued, "You have no right at the cannon's mouth to impose on an unwilling people your . . . notions of what is good." Others, such as Louisiana Democrat Donelson Caffery, claimed that imperialism undermined the American economy. Likewise, Booker T. Washington contended, "Until our nation has settled the Negro and Indian problems, I do not believe that we have a right to assume more social problems."[33] And yet Masters's antipathy toward imperialism proved grounded in beliefs particular to his understanding of the American past. Throughout his career, Masters idolized a Jeffersonian agrarian republic of localized economies and individual autonomy. Accordingly, leaders such as McKinley and Roosevelt—and before them, Chief Justice John Marshall and Alexander Hamilton—undermined the Revolutionary ideals that demanded freedom from distant rule, both politically and economically. In a direct violation of these principles, imperialism further drove the world into the hands of industrialists who imposed upon foreign populations the very injustices that Americans had once rebelled against. Inspired by the rhetoric of William Jennings Bryan, an anti-imperialist himself, Masters founded the Jefferson Club in Chicago in 1908 to advocate for Democrats who reflected Bryan's political proclivities.[34] Masters believed that aligning with this sentiment could return the Democratic Party, and the nation, to the Jeffersonian spirit that predated the Civil War.

However, the reality of Jeffersonian America, especially between the purchase of the Louisiana Territory in 1803 and the collapse of the Whig Party in the mid-1850s, represented one of the most expansive eras of conquest in U.S. history. By the end of this period, the United States had removed Native peoples from the southeastern part of the country (1831–38), defeated Mexico in a two-year war (1846–48), which resulted in the acquisition of territory stretching from the Rocky Mountains to the Pacific Ocean, and begun the settlement of territories west of the Mississippi. How does one reconcile Masters's admiration for this period of conquest—a period when a "frontier" of "pioneers" required the removal of Native peoples from their land—with his anti-imperialism?

For Masters, his grandfather provided the fundamental starting point for a nostalgic tale of American decline. According to family lore, Squire Davis Masters represented a generation of pioneers who, during the 1830s and 1840s, conquered and tamed the Illinois frontier for the sake of the independent farmer.[35] According to this myth, the conquest of the frontier was the actualization of the nation itself. Masters began his autobiography, *Across Spoon River*, by describing his family's legacy as pioneers and revering his grandfather for being a self-made gentleman farmer, comparing him, as a boy, to George Washington.[36] Masters also crafted characters in *Spoon River Anthology* that expressed his support of these pioneering ideals.[37] More broadly, the sentimental history of pioneering was in the air in the late nineteenth century. Frederick Jackson Turner famously celebrated the "frontier" in his speech on its significance to the formation of democracy, delivered at the World's Fair in Chicago during Masters's first summer in the city.[38] Charged with this sense of nostalgia and veneration for a lost American disposition, one now tainted and nearly erased by men like McKinley and Roosevelt, Masters wrote from an anti-imperialist stance that did not so much reject conquest as judge expansion according to who was doing the conquering and to what end. In Masters's reading of American history, the era of pioneering conquest before the Civil War was undertaken by the common people, a nation of independent farmers and artisans who assured the longevity of the Revolution's ideals. Overseas acquisitions after the Civil War, on the other hand, represented the apotheosis of corporate-industrial power in the postwar period and countered the pioneering ethos of Squire Davis's generation. This was exemplified by the purchase of Alaska (1868) as the first stepping stone toward east Asian markets, and the annexation of the Hawaiian Islands (1898) on the way to the Philippines, both of which were undertaken by Republican administrations.

For Masters, the Civil War marked a turning point in the values of the American elite. During and after Reconstruction, claimed Masters,

Republican officeholders, modeling themselves on Hamiltonian ambivalence toward democratic politics, fell into patterns that perpetuated the power of industrial capitalists at the expense of the common people. Masters saw this economic deceit as a "process of producing and distributing wealth" whose effects "have . . . struck at human liberty."[39] Despite a promise of equality enshrined in the Constitution, the American elite developed a system that fostered a period of unchecked power and influence, benefiting the wealthy few at the expense of the democratic mass. This development violated the fundamental vision of the nation's founders, who, according to Masters, were "a few free spirits . . . [who] set it to follow a career of justice to the common man upon a fresh soil."[40] For Masters, these "free spirits" settled the land as pioneers, not conquerors; they were regular Americans who embodied the nation's origins, a sentiment lost in modern times.

GRAVEYARD LEGACY

When Edgar Lee Masters found success in 1915 with the publication of *Spoon River Anthology*, very little trace of *The New Star Chamber* remained. In fact, while Masters was personally satisfied with the 1904 collection of essays, the public response was minimal, and the book largely dropped out of memory as soon as it appeared. However, although not polemical like *The New Star Chamber*, Masters's unexpectedly best-selling collection of poetry echoes his earlier book. In this regard, the epitaphs of Spoon River exhibit the unmistakable fingerprints of Masters's anti-imperialism, anti-elitism, and Populist sympathies.

Masters expressed a sense that the nation had abandoned its founding principles during the Civil War, and it appears in epitaphs like the one for Knowlt Hoheimer, a soldier who died at the Battle of Missionary Ridge after enlisting to avoid imprisonment. He laments,

Rather a thousand times the county jail
Than to lie under this marble figure with wings,
And this granite pedestal
Bearing the words, *"Pro Patria."*
What do they mean, anyway?[41]

Likewise, to Masters, a son and grandson of anti-Lincoln Copperheads who perceived the Civil War as the beginning of the nation's downfall, Jacob Goodpasture spoke for many when he "cried out in bitterness of soul: / 'O glorious republic now no more!'" when war erupted in 1861. To Goodpasture, his son's death in battle was "in a cause unjust! / In the strife of Freedom slain!"[42] Jefferson Howard, modeled on Masters's father, Hardin, "[h]ating slavery, but no less war," fights personal battles against the "Republicans, Calvinists, merchants, bankers, / Hating me, yet fearing my arm."[43] To Masters, Appomattox was the death of Jefferson's agrarian republic, now replaced by a system where power radiated outward from a federal center for the benefit of financial elites.

Several poems in *Spoon River Anthology* deal with Masters's disgust with a judicial system that played clear favorites. "John M. Church" is one such poem. Told as an epitaph for a corporate lawyer who "pulled the wires with judge and jury" to win cases against "the crippled, the widow and orphan," the ending of this poem makes clear Masters's opinion of people like Church: "But the rats devoured my heart / And a snake made a nest in my skull!"[44] Likewise, the Circuit Judge, watching his headstone and memory succumb to erosion, regrets deciding cases on technicalities rather than justice. His punishment

> Was to lie speechless, yet with vision clear,
> Seeing that even Hod Putt, the murderer,
> Hanged by my sentence,
> Was innocent in soul compared with me.[45]

Defenders of the downtrodden were victims as well. Carl Hamblin damns Justice for her blindness toward the poor:

> brandishing the sword,
> Sometimes striking a child, again a laborer,
> Again a slinking woman, again a lunatic.
> In her right hand she held a scale;
> Into the scale pieces of gold were tossed
> By those who dodged the strokes of the sword.[46]

Also, the town fathers are quick to bring Daisy Fraser before the court to fine her "ten dollars and costs," but to her, Editor Whedon, the circuit judge, and the reverends are prostitutes as well, willing to sell their virtue to the highest bidder.[47] These feelings can also be found throughout *The New Star Chamber* as Masters argues that the judiciary acted as the legitimizing arm of a newly imperial, oligarchic America.

Likewise, epitaphs such as Yee Bow's and Wendell P. Bloyd's express disdain for the hypocritical moralism that Masters criticizes throughout *The New Star Chamber*. The Christian townspeople of Spoon River force Yee Bow into Sunday school "and tried to get me to drop Confucius for Jesus." While at school,

Harry Wiley,
The minister's son, caved my ribs into my lungs,
With a blow of his fist.[48]

Wendell Bloyd was committed to an asylum for his vocal apostasy and was beaten to death by a guard for saying that "God lied to Adam, and destined him / To lead the life of a fool."[49] These lines serve as a severe condemnation of violence perpetrated by those who called themselves Christians. In "Deacon Taylor," Masters criticizes the private hypocrisy of public moralism. Taylor was a member of the church and a prohibitionist but admits in death that

For every noon for thirty years,
I slipped behind the prescription partition
In Trainor's drug store
And poured a generous drink
From the bottle marked *"Spiritus frumenti."*[50]

In *The New Star Chamber*, the frustration at hypocritical moralism is prevalent, especially in "Theodore Roosevelt," where "Mr. Roosevelt's advice to speak softly but carry a big stick, his admonitions to avoid ignoble ease, to stand for civic righteousness, to back our words with deeds and to couple Christian principles with resolute courage sound hollow and puerile" against the facts of his personal bombast and

America's willingness to occupy weaker nations.[51] To Masters, those who would dictate morals to others threatened the rights of all and often failed to live up to the standards they created.

Overall, *Spoon River Anthology* was received well both by critics and by the reading public and garnered fame and attention for Masters, whose works were unsuccessful before and after the publication of his famous fictional epitaphs.[52] On the other hand, while *The New Star Chamber* was released to reviews that "gratified [Masters] exceedingly," sales were disappointing.[53] Masters admitted its negligible impact in retrospect, as the book is directly referenced only twice in his 1936 autobiography. Likewise, *Lincoln: The Man*, published sixteen years after *Spoon River Anthology*, was so poorly received that it is mentioned only once in the autobiography. Despite over two decades passing between *Spoon River Anthology* and *Across Spoon River*, the autobiography contains little from Masters's life after 1915. To the literary world, and in a sense to Masters himself, *Spoon River Anthology* was the shining publication of his writing life; everything else faded. However, by imparting his ideology onto the deceased of Spoon River, Masters saved his ideas from the historical graveyard and ensured that the spirit of *The New Star Chamber* lived on.

Notes

1. Edgar Lee Masters, *Across Spoon River: An Autobiography* (New York: Farrar and Rinehart, 1936), 78.

2. Masters, 60.

3. Masters, 404.

4. Herbert K. Russell, *Edgar Lee Masters: A Biography* (Urbana and Chicago: University of Illinois Press, 2001), 38.

5. Masters, *Across Spoon River*, xii.

6. Russell, *Edgar Lee Masters*, 323.

7. Russell, 48.

8. E. Anthony Rotundo, "Learning about Manhood: Gender Ideals and the Middle-Class Family in Nineteenth-Century America," in *Manliness and Morality: Middle-Class Masculinity in Britain and America, 1800–1940*, eds. J. A. Mangan and James Walvan (Manchester: Manchester University Press, 1987), 35–52.

9. Michael S. Kimmel, *Manhood in America: A Cultural History* (Oxford: Oxford University Press, 2018), 30.

10. Russell, *Edgar Lee Masters*, 117.

11. Russell, 278–79.

12. John D. Hicks, *The Populist Revolt: A History of the Farmers' Alliance and the People's Party* (Lincoln: University of Nebraska Press, 1931).

13. Russell, *Edgar Lee Masters*, 48–50.

14. Richard Hofstadter, *The Age of Reform: From Bryan to F.D.R.* (New York: Alfred A. Knopf, 1955).

15. Charles Postel, *The Populist Vision* (New York: Oxford University Press, 2009).

16. Russell, *Edgar Lee Masters*, 13–14, 179.

17. See Postel, *Populist Vision*, 103–37, 269–75.

18. Masters, *Across Spoon River*, 56.

19. Masters, 209.

20. As quoted in Russell, *Edgar Lee Masters*, 47.

21. For an excellent overview of the Progressive Era and Progressive politics, see Michael McGerr, *A Fierce Discontent: The Rise and Fall of the Progressive Movement in America, 1870– 1920* (Oxford: Oxford University Press, 2003). Older but still highly influential is Hofstadter, *Age of Reform*. For a review of Progressivism as an idea or political philosophy, see Bradley C. S. Watson, *Progressivism: The Strange History of a Radical Idea* (Notre Dame, IN: University of Notre Dame Press, 2020).

22. See Martin J. Sklar, *The Corporate Reconstruction of American Capitalism, 1890–1916: The Market, the Law, and Politics* (New York: Cambridge University Press, 1988).

23. McGerr, *Fierce Discontent*, 149. For more on consumerism during this period, see Kristin L. Hoganson, *Consumers' Imperium: The Global Production of American Domesticity, 1865–1920* (Chapel Hill: University of North Carolina Press, 2007).

24. See Michael Mark Cohen, *The Conspiracy of Capital: Law, Violence, and American Popular Radicalism in the Age of Monopoly* (Boston: University of Massachusetts Press, 2019).

25. For more on Masters's anti-Republican, and particularly anti-Lincoln, views, see Matthew D. Norman, "An Illinois Iconoclast: Edgar Lee Masters and the Anti-Lincoln Tradition," *Journal of the Abraham Lincoln Association* 24, no. 1 (Winter 2003): 43–57.

26. See, for example, Lincoln Steffens, *The Shame of the Cities* (New York: McClure, Phillips and Co., 1904).

27. McGerr, *Fierce Discontent*, 56.

28. McGerr, 47–54, 107–14.

29. Russell, *Edgar Lee Masters*, 51–52.

30. Postel, *Populist Vision*, 161.

31. Quoted in David H. Burton, "Theodore Roosevelt: Confident Imperialist," *Review of Politics* 23, no. 3 (1961): 356–57.

32. Fred H. Harrington, "The Anti-Imperialist Movement in the United States, 1898–1900," *Mississippi Valley Historical Review* 22, no. 2 (September 1935): 211.

33. All quotes from David J. Silbey, *A War of Frontier and Empire: The Phillippine-American War, 1899–1902* (New York: Hill and Wang, 2007), 89.

34. Jason Stacy, *Spoon River America: Edgar Lee Masters and the Myth of the American Small Town* (Urbana: University of Illinois Press, 2021), 60.

35. Masters recounts his grandfather's service during the Blackhawk War (1832) in *Across Spoon River*, 5.

36. Masters, 4–5.

37. Stacy, *Spoon River America*, 82.

38. Stacy, 55–56.

39. Edgar Lee Masters, *The New Star Chamber and Other Essays* (Chicago: Hammersmark, 1904), 9.

40. Edgar Lee Masters, *Lincoln: The Man* (New York: Dodd, Mead, 1931), 495–96.

41. Edgar Lee Masters, *Spoon River Anthology* (New York: Macmillan, 1919), 27.

42. Masters, 46.

43. Masters, 96.

44. Masters, 85.

45. Masters, 75.

46. Masters, 130–31.

47. Masters, 20.

48. Masters, 101.

49. Masters, 81.

50. Masters, 58.

51. Masters, *New Star Chamber and Other Essays*, 29.

52. Stacy, *Spoon River America*, 97.

53. Edgar Lee Masters, *Across Spoon River: An Autobiography* (Urbana and Chicago, IL: University of Illinois Press, 1991), 276-77.

To My Father, Hardin Wallace Masters

NOTE

Several of the essays in this book were published during the campaign of 1900, or within a short time after. Many of them relate to the imperial policy of the United States which grew out of the war with Spain. These essays preserve, to some extent, the thought which was current during a portion of the development of that policy; and may therefore have an historical value, even if they do not profoundly discuss the constitutional questions at issue.

Others of these essays have never before been published; among which the one entitled "Implied Powers and Imperialism" was designed to go so thoroughly into the fallacy upon which imperialism rests that the essays upon the Philippine question might be constitutionally rounded out. If this book shall prove in any manner to be a contribution to the literature of liberty, I shall feel that the time and the labor of its composition were not wasted.

E. L. M.

The New Star Chamber

I F it be remembered that positive law and judicial interpretation proceed from the ebb or flow of human emotions no difficulty can be encountered in explaining those revivals of regulations and restrictions which preceding ages have repudiated.[1] Human nature undoubtedly improves and may always be capable of improvement. But human nature in its essential passions remains constituent and integral. Below these passions are human needs which produce activities of all sorts to obtain the means of life. And this is the rudimentary spring of human action out of which the whole drama of life is produced. As these needs are gratified or repressed; or in brief, as the economic question is regarded so are the laws framed and administered. If in the production of wealth the laws are unequal and if in its distribution the laws are unequal, the administration of these laws must preserve the inequality so established. And so out of the process of acquiring and holding land and personal property; and out of the process of producing and distributing wealth have arisen those laws which struck at human liberty.

And at the bottom of these we perceive the play of human passion. Particular desires may exhaust themselves, or be eradicated; others may meet with counter desires and sink into deeper channels only to arise in a succeeding century clothed in some other form. But whenever powerful factions renew the same ends the means of their attainment are likely to be of the same character as those employed before.

What prophetic insight had the author of that apothegm which reads "The love of money is the root of all evil."[2] It is the love of money which strikes at liberty to cripple the economic power of men; and it is the love of money which resorts to dissimulation in order to obscure the campaign that is being waged. For liberty was never attacked under the banner of despotism; but always under the banner of liberty. Religious and political persecutions and the sanguinary administration of internal government have always held aloft the standard of liberty, or the general welfare. Nor is it remarkable now that the sponsors of the "labor injunction"[3] should urge in its defense its efficacy in preserving the liberty of the employer to hire whom he pleases; and the liberty of all men to obtain work without molestation. This is the out-worn sophistry of kings and the complaint and ferocious magistrates who did their will. The labor injunction is what Lord Tennyson[4] called a "new-old revolution." It is the skeleton of the Star Chamber drawing about its tattered cerements the banner of a free people and masking its face with a similitude of the republic. The labor injunction is insidious and plausible. It speaks the language of liberty. It disarms criticism because brought into use in times of disorder; and because it avows nothing but salutary purposes. It has put itself upon such a footing that the irrelevant conclusion is drawn against its enemies that because they are opposed to it they must be opposed to law and order; while those who favor it are the friends of law and order. So that, as in many similar instances, people forget that to overthrow the law to punish a breach of the law is to meet anarchy with anarchy itself. Why should not the lawful way already provided be followed in the punishment of wrong? The spirit which advocates the lawless labor injunction is the same essential spirit which animates the mob. This spirit cannot successfully hide itself behind the high sounding acclaims of law and order. It will be ultimately dragged to the light for every eye to see. When that time shall arrive the fact will be recognized that the same tyrannical purpose which erected the Star Chamber, turned a court of chancery[5] into an engine of lawless power.

Mr. Hallam,[6] who wrote most authoritatively of the English Constitution, said that the course of proceeding in the Star Chamber "seems to have nearly resembled that of the chancery." But observe that the same reasoning which supported the Star Chamber fortifies the chancery court to-day in the use of the labor injunction. The Star Chamber was established to secure good government. The chancery court has resorted to the process of injunction to secure good government. The Star Chamber's powers were directed towards preventing riots and unlawful assemblies. The labor injunction of a chancery court is issued to prevent riots and unlawful assemblies. In the Star Chamber there was no indictment. In the chancery court there is no indictment. In the Star Chamber there were no witnesses, and the evidence was produced in writing and read to the council. So in the chancery court in the trial of contempt for violating the injunction there are no witnesses but the evidence is produced in writing and read to the chancellor. In the Star Chamber there was no trial by jury. In the chancery court there is no trial by jury. In the Star Chamber the council could inflict any punishment short of death, and frequently sentenced objects of its wrath to the pillory, to whipping and to the cutting off of ears. In the chancery court the chancellor may inflict any punishment short of death or imprisonment in the penitentiary, subject to vague limitations arising from inference, and subject to the discretion of a reviewing court. With each embarrassment to arbitrary power the Star Chamber became emboldened to undertake further usurpation. And with each necessity of monopoly the chancery courts have proceeded to meet the necessity. The Star Chamber finally summoned juries before it for verdicts disagreeable to the government, and fined and imprisoned them. It spread terrorism among those who were called to do constitutional acts. It imposed ruinous fines. It became the chief defence of Charles[7] against assaults upon those usurpations which cost him his life. From the beginning it defied Magna Charta[8] in denying jury-trial, in forcing men to incriminate themselves, or what is scarcely less repugnant to reason, to manifest their innocence. While to-day the chancery courts defy the written constitution of the states and of the federal government in denying jury trials and forcing men to incriminate themselves or to manifest their innocence. At last with the inhuman punishment administered by it to Prynn, Burton and Bastwick,[9] the people long cultivated by the constitutional lawyers of England procured its abolition. Can the chancery courts of this country expect to escape appropriate discipline when the time shall arrive that the eyes of the people shall see that these courts have habitually over-ridden the laws of the land?

For, be it understood, the chancery court in its inception was a regal invention? Its powers, its practices, its code are of pure consuetudinary growth. It began by interfering, through the king himself, with the administration of the law by the regularly constituted courts. It began weak. It grew strong by silent and gradual encroachment. Its suitors multiplied until the king committed its control to his chancellor. Its decisions have always depended upon the conscience of the chancellor. While pretending to limit itself to subjects not triable in the law courts, or where the law courts afforded an inadequate remedy, it grew to take cognizance of matters which were clearly triable by a jury. There has been serious conflict between the chancery courts and the law courts from the time of Sir Edward Coke[10] to this day. But notwithstanding doubts as to the precise powers of the chancery courts it is perfectly sure that they never had jurisdiction of crimes; or to pass upon torts;[11] or trespasses, except under very limited regulations; and never in short had jurisdiction to pass upon any subject where the law courts furnished an adequate remedy, or where jury trial was a necessitous and constitutional mode of examination. For a chancery court is not equipped with a jury. Hence where it assumes to adjudicate subjects outside of the domain of its jurisdiction, jury trial falls, not because it has gone outside of its sphere as to the subject, but because it has retreated into its sphere as to the procedure. This is all that can be made out of a refusal of a jury trial in contempt proceedings. It is rare dissimulation which countenances a theft of jurisdiction on one hand, but insists upon the other hand in a strict regard for the jurisdictional method of dealing with the subject matter after the theft. The man who stole meat but refused to eat it on Friday is the analogue of the chancery court which denies a jury trial of a charge of disobeying a labor injunction, on the ground that a jury trial is not an adjunct of a chancery court.

Now as to the subject-matter of the extraordinary injunctions resorted to by the chancery courts in the last decade it must never be forgotten that it is purely economic. Between the employer and the employe [sic] the essential question is economic. The employer wants labor cheap; the employe wants it dear. The conflict between these desires is an aspect of industrial competition. When these desires cannot be compromised into harmony the result is a strike. We then have the following history of things preceding the issuance of a labor injunction: First a dissatisfaction on the part of the laborers with their wages or terms of employment, which may be well or ill founded; second, a simultaneous quitting by the laborers of their employment; third, some of these laborers go into the streets, in behalf of all, to notify other men who would take the places deserted that there is a strike and why it was resorted to, and to circulate hand-bills[12] requesting men not to take the old places and thus break the strike. There may be clashes on the street resulting from all the countless circumstances which attend a time of inflamed feelings. And fourth, the employer either cannot get any help, or can get so little help that his business is stopped. Now, to analyze the character of these acts it is obvious that no law forbids any man from being dissatisfied with his terms of employment, whether he does so reasonably or unreasonably. No law forbids a man or body of men from quitting their work either singly or in a body. No law prevents men from being in the streets. No law prevents them from talking, or from circulating hand-bills which contain no malicious defamation. So far then every act done is legal. If these men resort to violence or crime of any sort then they are amenable to a good many different laws—but only in a criminal court and not in a court of chancery. But the labor injunction which follows upon the development of the foregoing conditions gathers under its inhibition two general classes of acts. It forbids the commission of crimes and torts because they injure the employer's business. The injury to business is coupled with the crime to dodge the law already referred to that the chancery courts have no jurisdiction over crimes. It forbids the doing of innocent acts like talking, circulating hand-bills and being on the street, because they are said to be the component acts of a conspiracy to injure the employer's business. Thus innocent acts are interdicted; thus conspiracies are interdicted; although conspiracies are crimes of which, as shown, a court of chancery has no jurisdiction. And so innocent acts are interdicted because they relate to the commission of a crime—the alleged conspiracy—and the crime—the alleged conspiracy—is interdicted because it injures business. This is precisely the sort of juggling that the patrons of the Star Chamber employed.

But does the fact that a crime injures business furnish legal warrant for enjoining[13] its commission? Burglary, larceny, arson, forgery,
cheating, counterfeiting and many other crimes injure business just as
much as a strike does; and yet no one pretends that these crimes can
be enjoined by a court of chancery. Such a pretense violently incurs the
organic law which has thrown about every man charged with crime
the right to have it specifically set out in an indictment; to meet the
witnesses face to face, and to have the question of fact of his guilt or
innocence passed upon by a jury. But if a court of chancery enjoin the
crime and some one is supposed to have committed it the chancery court
insists upon trying the man charged upon affidavits and without a jury.
Hence courts of chancery either have no power to enjoin such things, or
having enjoined them must proceed in dealing with them according to
the constitution relating to such subjects. If courts of chancery cannot in
dealing with such things afford indictments, witnesses and juries then
it cannot have power to deal with them at all; because the constitution
provides for an indictment, for confrontation of the witnesses and for
jury trial in the most absolute terms. And to say that a court of chancery
may enjoin crimes which injure business, is to say that it has jurisdiction
of all crimes against the rights of property and of all crimes which
indirectly affect property rights, which is absurd. No one carries the
argument that far. For if it should be carried that far then the criminal
courts would yield to the chancery courts, and the constitution would
be so palpably nullified that no one could be befooled on the subject.
So then, to recapitulate, the chancery courts have no power over crimes
of themselves; they have no power over crimes because they injure
business, for the incident of injury to business is not distinctive of those
acts prohibited by labor injunctions, but pertains to many crimes and
wrongs; and therefore nothing has been added to the crime itself which
gives the chancery court power over it. On this point the defender of
labor injunctions must either show that the offenses prohibited by labor
injunctions are peculiar in their injury to business or property interests;
or he must admit that such injury flows from a great variety of offenses
and so be carried by the force of the admission to the manifest absurdity of asserting that the chancery court may enjoin burglary, larceny,
swindling and other crimes. This dilemma leads the defender of the

labor injunction to say that while the vitality of the injunction depends upon the theory that the act enjoined is a crime, still that the court does not punish one who has violated a labor injunction for a crime, but for disobedience of the injunction of the court. That is, if men are enjoined from prosecuting a conspiracy and are found guilty of having done so, the court in fining and imprisoning them does so not for having prosecuted the conspiracy but for having prosecuted the conspiracy in disobedience of the court's order. Usurpation and hypocrisy have never been more thinly veiled. A punishment in contempt proceedings for having violated a labor injunction must be either for having done a wrongful act, or for having done a wrongful act in disobedience of a court's inhibition. For an act which is meritorious[14] or lawful can be done by any one in spite of a court's inhibition not to do it. If the court should seek to punish one for doing a meritorious or a lawful act a complete defense to the prosecution would be that the act was lawful or meritorious; and the court could not punish for mere disobedience of an order forbidding the doing of such lawful or meritorious act. No one can deny that if a court has forbidden what the law does not forbid it should and must expect to be contemned. So that as no injunction is worth while unless lawful punishment can be inflicted for disobeying it, the injunction must forbid something which the law forbids, such as the crime of conspiracy. Now if conspiracy were a meritorious thing it would, as shown, be useless to enjoin it, for if it were enjoined it might be done with impunity. It is because conspiracy is wrong that the general law of contempt can be argued to warrant summary punishment where a conspiracy is carried on in the face of an injunction. Is the punishment for the disobedience of the injunction? This cannot be true. Because the doing of a legal act, though enjoined, cannot be punished as a contempt. Therefore disobedience of an injunction of itself cannot be punished as a contempt. It therefore results that the thing punished is the crime. The disobedience is an invention of a dissembling jurisprudence. It is one of those fictions of law in which Anglo-Saxon jurisprudence has been absurdly and injuriously prolific. But the disobedience is not essential. The invariable element is the wrongfulness of the act. The crime or wrong is the basis of disobedience. It is the substance of the disobedience. It interpenetrates the disobedience, however, the subject is viewed.

Generally speaking labor injunctions enjoin the commission of crimes. But this may be stated in another way. They enjoin crimes, such as assaults; and they enjoin innocent acts like talking and being in the streets; because, it is alleged, these innocent acts are done pursuant to a combination to injure the employer's business. So the combination, that is, the "conspiracy," is enjoined; and likewise all acts innocent or otherwise, done in prosecution of the "conspiracy." Comprehensively speaking the labor injunction covers crimes; and essentially speaking it concerns itself with what is called a "conspiracy." The invention of "conspiracy" as applied to strikes is in line with the whole policy of monopoly which quotes scripture for a purpose. Admitting for the time that a combination of men to secure better wages is a conspiracy the charge comes with poor grace from that side of the world which has been in a league against popular rights and equal laws from the dawn of history. So long ago as 1776 Adam Smith[15] declared that masters are everywhere in a tacit but constant and united combination not to raise wages above their actual rate. Is this not the undeniable truth today? John Stuart Mill[16] denounced the labor laws of Elizabeth's[17] reign, passed by a parliament of employers as evincing the infernal spirit of the slave driver. But these injunctions are nothing but a form of labor laws directed to the point of keeping down the rate of wages. Every tariff act is the result of a confederation of manufacturers; and every tariff act injures the business of those who make the tariff profitable. Yet there is no charge of conspiracy and no injunction concerning it. Combinations of capital and the consolidation of corporations injure the business of those who are thereby more effectually preyed upon; yet there is no charge of conspiracy and no injunction concerning these things. Employers are leagued together to-day under various deceptive names for the purpose of dominating labor. To do this they have contributed large amounts to a common treasury to be used in court proceedings and in legislative halls against labor. This injures the business of the laborer; and yet there is no charge of conspiracy and no injunction concerning it. The Philippine conquest[18] was the result of a compact among the trusts to get trade; and this hurts the business of all not interested; and yet there is no charge of conspiracy as to this! What ethical gnat are these patrons of law and order straining at who conjure with the word "conspiracy" when men strike for better wages? What ethical camels have they not swallowed? What burdens have they not imposed growing out of their "conspiracies" and which they have not moved with one of their fingers?

Nevertheless and in spite of all objections the courts have uniformly held that workingmen may combine for the purpose of bettering their condition. That a body of men may at will, wisely or unwisely, cease their relations with an employer; that they may maintain a peaceable picket and employ peaceable persuasion directed toward preventing men from taking service with the employer. But if these allowable acts inflict injury upon the employers then it is said that the allowable acts become unlawful. They become a conspiracy; because, it is held, that they are done for the purpose of inflicting injury which is an unlawful end. No account is taken of the fact that the ulterior end of the strike is to obtain better wages and that the injury is inflicted as an instrumentality. So that if men for the purpose of bettering their own condition and in the line of labor competition may not inflict injury upon their employer, then the situation simply is, that they may strike, that is, cease to work; but only when it does not injure their employer. But if the ceasing to work does not injure their employer then the employer will be indifferent thereto, and the men must eat whatever bread is given them. On the contrary if the ceasing to work does injure the employer then such act, according to the employer, becomes unlawful. So, it is seen, that in either of these situations the employer is given the whole field of benefit and power and the men are reduced to a condition of industrial impotence. This is the whole of the argument. But while such restrictions upon the conduct of laborers result from the premise of the injury to the employer's business, the employer is held to be privileged to hire whom he pleases and to discriminate against whom he pleases. His discrimination consists in retiring the strikers from the labor market by an injunction; and his privilege follows after when the field is occupied by men who for one reason or another will work at the master's price. Freedom to give work at our own price and freedom to you to obtain work, but only at our price, has been the creed of the monopolist from all times.

Limiting the discussion to a combination of men who do lawful acts which injure the employer and induce him to capitulate and grant the wages asked, it may be pertinently asked what law can be invoked to interfere with such a form of competition? Every merchant is engaged in injuring the business of his competitor. Every advertisement is a persuasion addressed to buyers to forsake one merchant and to deal with the advertiser. Every lowering of price of commodities for sale is an injury to those who have them for sale and who must likewise lower the price or lose custom. Every simplification of production, every elimination of waste, every combination of faculties or devices by which trade is secured injures the business of those to whom these expedients are impossible. The whole domain of traffic under the competitive system is interpenetrated with injury to some and benefit to others. Long hours and low wages injure the business of the laborer. Pauper[19] labor injures the business of the citizen laborer. Leagues of employers inspired by the policy of controlling the labor market injure the business of the laborer. Lock-outs resorted to by employers whether as the result of combination or otherwise injure the business of the laborers. Is it possible then that laborers may not in the course of competition compel their employers to raise wages and lower hours or to accede to any regulation lawful in itself by which wages and hours of service may be presently established and secured for the future? If men can only strike and retire from the competitive field and go elsewhere for work then the employer is relieved of competition.

By organization and the use of courts he has abolished that competition by which he would have to pay higher wages and suffer injury in his business; and has taken the high ground where he can pay low wages without competition and injure the business of the laborers. This is the ultimate substance of the question, stripped of its pretense and its sophistry.

Yet some one asks what shall be done if strikers resort to violence and assaults; if they intimidate and riot and destroy property? This is a simple question. The criminal code expressly prohibits such things, and if they are done the criminal courts will and should punish them. But the very reason that the criminal courts are not resorted to while the chancery courts are is precisely because the employer wants to be assisted in his economic struggle; and is either personally indifferent to these acts except as they bear upon the economic question, or because these acts are not done so extensively or so often as represented. Nero[20] burned Rome and charged the Christians with it. And this subterfuge has been practiced always as a tactical move in a campaign of extermination. For nothing relaxes objection and silences criticism upon usurpation so much as the creation of a condition which strengthens the "Must-do-something" policy. Nothing has helped the employer so much in the plainly lawless and forbidden use of the writ of injunction as that condition of violence which he so loudly deplores. Does the employer produce this condition himself? It has been proven in some cases that he does. But whether he does or not the argument that the constitution in all its requirements should be supported and jealously preserved is not in the least affected. The only hope of liberty is a conscientious regard for its canons, most of which are expressed in the written Constitution of the Republic and the State Republics.

Notes

1. An English court from 1487 to 1641 that was established to ensure enforcement of the law against powerful individuals who may not have been convicted in ordinary courts. However, it has been more associated with corruption, arbitrary rulings, and no due process. See Edward P. Cheyney, "The Court of Star Chamber," *American Historical Review* 18, no. 4 (1913): 727–50.

2. 1 Timothy 6:10 (King James Version).

3. "An order or writ issued by a court of equity commanding an individual or group of individuals to do or refrain from doing certain acts." Robert M. Debevec, "The Labor Injunction: Weapon or Tool," *Cleveland State Law Review* 4, no. 2 (1955): 102.

4. Alfred Tennyson (1809–92), poet laureate (1850–92) during the Victorian era. See John H. Baker, *An Introduction to English Legal History* (Oxford: Oxford University Press, 2019).

5. A court in England and Wales that offered an alternative to common law. While common law was often perceived as slow, the chancery courts often proved efficient, though prone to high-handedness. See Baker, *Introduction*.

6. Henry Hallam (1777–1859), an English historian whose famous work, *The Constitutional History of England* (1827), covers constitutional history from the accession of Henry VII to the accession of George III. See Peter Clark, *Henry Hallam* (Boston: Twayne, 1982).

7. King Charles I of England (1600–49) ruled England from 1629 until his execution in 1649. See Richard Cust, *Charles I: A Political Life* (Harlow, UK: Pearson Longman, 2007).

8. Signed by the English king John in 1215 under threat of civil war, this document declared the ruler to be subject to the rule of law and documented the liberties held by the large landholders of England. In the eighteenth century the document became increasingly perceived as guaranteeing the rights of all English people. See Peter Linebaugh, *The Magna Carta Manifesto: Liberties and Commons for All* (Berkeley: University of California Press, 2009).

9. Henry Burton, John Bastwick, and William Prynne were charged in March 1637 in the Star Chamber for publishing books criticizing King Charles I and the Church of England. See Christine Reese, "Controlling Print? Burton, Bastwick, and Prynne and the Politics of Memory" (Ph.D. diss., Pennsylvania State University, 2007), 1.

10. Edward Coke (1552–1634), English judge and politician, served during the Elizabethan and Jacobean periods. See Baker, *Introduction*.

11. "Any wrong or injury; a wrongful act, for which an action will lie; a form of action, in some States, for a wrong or injury." William Wheeler Thornton, ed., *The Universal Cyclopaedia of Law: A Practical Compendium of Legal Information . . .* (Long Island: Edward Thompson, 1885), 2:1234.

12. "A written or printed notice displayed to inform those concerned of something to be done." John Bouvier, *Law Dictionary Adapted to the Constitution* (Philadelphia: J. B. Lippincott, 1883), 741.

13. "To put an injunction on, direct with authority, order or to prohibit or restrain by a judicial order or decree." *Webster's Practical Dictionary* (Springfield, MA: G. & C. Merriam Co., 1906), s.v. "enjoin."

14. "Deserving thanks; worthy of gratitude." *Webster's Practical Dictionary*, s.v. "meritorious."

15. Adam Smith (1723–90), Scottish political economist and philosopher, best known for his book *The Wealth of Nations*. G. R. Bassiry and Marc Jones, "Adam Smith and the Ethics of Contemporary Capitalism," *Journal of Business Ethics* 12, no. 8 (1993): 621–27.

16. John Stuart Mill (1806–73), English economist, conceived of liberty as justifying the freedom of the individual in opposition to unlimited state and social control. See Emile Thouverez, *John Stuart Mill* (Paris: Bloud & Cie, 1908).

17. Elizabeth I (1533–1603) reigned during a period of English expansion and colonization. See Allison Weir, *The Life of Elizabeth I* (New York: Random House, 2013).

18. The Philippine-American War (1899–1902), conflict of occupation and insurgency in which the first Philippine republic fought occupation by the United States. See David J. Silbey, *A War of Frontier and Empire: The Philippine-American War, 1899–1902* (New York: Hill and Wang, 2007).

19. "A poor person; esp., one so indigent as to depend on charity for maintenance; one supported by public provision." *Webster's Practical Dictionary*, s.v. "pauper."

20. Nero Claudius Caesar Augustus Germanicus (AD 37–68), fifth emperor of Rome known for his tyranny. He was originally blamed for the fire but used Christians as a scapegoat to remove suspicion from himself. Edward Champlin, "Nero Reconsidered," *New England Review* 19, no. 2 (1998): 97–108.

THEODORE ROOSEVELT

THE rise of Mr. Roosevelt to the presidency of the United States brought into the arena of world interests a third figure similar in temperament and imagination to two others who had before his time occupied conspicuous places in current history. In poetry, in philosophy and in statesmanship movements are distinguished by schools of men who are animated by the same inspiration. Germany furnishes the illustration of Goethe[1] and Schiller;[2] France that of Voltaire and Rousseau; England that of Fox, Pitt and Burke, and later, in poetry, that of Shelley, Byron and Coleridge. In America, Emerson, Alcott, Thoreau and Margaret Fuller developed the transcendental philosophy; while in statesmanship we associate upon general principles the names of Jefferson, Madison and Monroe; or those of Webster and Clay.

The tide of imperialism did not reach America until the war with Spain was concluded. Its waters had lapped the foundations of other governments long before; and even in America discerning intellects saw the drift of the current as early as the war between the states. That war elevated a school of political thinkers who placed government above men and who were bewitched with those policies of special privilege which centralized the government and prepared it for the final step. Mr. McKinley nevertheless may be said to have ended the line of the familiar school of American presidents. His physical appearance was of that character for which the people are accustomed to look in the selection of their presidents. His manner and his speech were modeled after the presidential type. And yet he bore some resemblance to Augustus Caesar. Like the latter, Mr. McKinley was a dissembler; he was plausible; he was crafty. He kept the people convinced that no change was being made in their government even in the face of apparent facts. But with the rise of Mr. Roosevelt the transformation was no longer concealed which had been obscured by the platitudes and the pious fallacies of his predecessor. Mr. Roosevelt obtrudes his imperial plans and preferences instead of hiding them. His demagoguery consists in appeals to the brutal tendencies in man, through slouch hat[3] and clanking spur and through crude familiarities with soldiers and policemen. Yet in this apparel he is as far from, the presidential figure as possible. The cropped-hair, the nose-glasses with the flying thread attached, the facial mannerisms and eccentricities place him apart from the dignified and courtly school of Buchanan, Garfield, Cleveland, Harrison or McKinley. If Mr. Roosevelt's successor shall wear a monocle and lead a pug dog, we ought not to marvel.[4]

When Mr. Roosevelt became president both what he was himself and what the times were, made it entirely appropriate that he should take his place beside Mr. Kipling and Emperor William.[5] These three men are the product of the same mood of nature. They are moved by the same ideals, if those convictions can be called such which lead men into the ways of vulgarity and violence. Mr. Kipling was reared in the most extensive, as well as the most despotic dependency of Great Britain. He had drunk to the full at the fountain of blood and gold. The history of Great Britain's dominion over India is one of chicane and murder, hypocrisy and plunder. Mr. Kipling's mind became filled with the images of military bluster and the principles of military honor. Scenes that would have convulsed the soul of Milton or Byron afforded him the material for casuistical doggerel. And by the strength of his imagination and because of a peculiar genius for popular appeal he filled the world with the echoes of the music hall, the barracks and the brothel. His songs brought poetry down to the level of the prize ring, the cock-pit and the racing stable. He became the de facto laureate[6] of England. So that butchery, oppression, and what hypocrites call destiny, acquired a glamour that thrilled the hearts of those who would have been horrified at these things in their visible forms. At last, at an opportune time, he sealed his hold upon the religious world by an anthropomorphic poem entitled "Recessional," in which the Diety is made to do duty as a military overseer for the armies of Great Britain, wherever they are engaged in planting the banner of empire.[7] In brief, Mr. Kipling is the laureate of strenuosity, and has done as much to corrupt the tastes and the manners of the world as any man who has lived in a hundred years. Emperor William approaches Mr. Roosevelt on many more sides than does Mr. Kipling. Emperor William is also strenuous; but he pretends to be what Mr. Roosevelt desires to have believed of himself, namely, that he is many-minded and triumphant in several fields of endeavor. The emperor aspires to be a writer, an orator, an artist, a poet, an architect, a savant, a hunter, a military genius; and he is some of these things to a degree as well as an emperor. All of these things may be said of Mr. Roosevelt, besides some others along the same line. For Mr. Roosevelt can wrestle, box, fence, ride and shoot as well as write histories and biographies; make speeches and win battles. He is a mixture of Caesar and Commodus;[8] and the vaunted resolution with which he took up the Philippine problem in 1901,[9] and the stringency with which it was carried out, shows that he is not averse to the effusion of blood when it is drawn in a patriotic cause. Neither was Tiberius, whose causes were always patriotic or justifiable. These three spirits, then, may be said either together or successively to have controlled the surface of the world's movement for a time; for now their power seems to be on the wane. But Mr. Roosevelt is different from his compeers in the point that he had a period of idealism in the early part of his career which neither Emperor William nor Mr. Kipling, so far as known, ever had.

But first as to his strenuosity it seems to be a reaction from physical feebleness. He has accentuated the attributes of courage, endurance and physical power for the reason that they were not natural to him, but have been acquired. The man who is born strong is not more self-conscious of his strength than the man who is born with sound limbs and faculties is self-conscious of these. But the man who is born weak and who has acquired strength is proud of his achievement and is self-conscious of it. Sedulous self-development has caused Mr. Roosevelt to emphasize

the physical life. Nothing with him counts for so much as power of endurance, the audacity to encounter danger, physical contest, the animal
in man and their capacity to greatly propagate themselves. Ordinarily
these feelings pass away with the period of adolescence, when the first
rush of blood has subsided from the head. But Mr. Roosevelt has carried
them over into his mature years and exploits them as peculiar wonders
characteristic of himself. This is the meaning of the strenuous life.
Amidst such tumultuous passions the writing of books is a pastime. The
warfare against civic wrong and for civic righteousness must be waged
with grim determination, with set teeth and scowling countenance.
But at all events the courage and the strenuosity with which the attack
is made must be emphasized more than the merit of the onslaught or
the righteousness of the cause. Mr. Roosevelt's advice to speak softly
but carry a big stick, his admonitions to avoid ignoble ease, to stand
for civic righteousness, to back our words with deeds and to couple
Christian principles with resolute courage sound hollow and puerile.[10]
There is too much of cruelty and tyranny in his self-vaunted courage.
His pompous poses, his spectacular manner, and his exhibitions of
power on all occasions suggest the strong little boy of the school yard,
who, by a fair measure of strength and a large measure of fortune, is
able greatly to his own delight to cow the feelings of his associates.

But if a man possess courage how shall he use it? If he possess great
energy of mind in what channels shall he direct it? What are courage
and ability of themselves? Of what consequence is the strenuous life
for its own sake? The world has seen its share of men who had courage
on the wrong side and who were strenuous in behalf of the strong
and wicked. Mr. Roosevelt's civic righteousness consists in straining at
gnats. He is very much concerned about the vices of people and about
crimes as well, if they happen to he committed by those with whom
he is socially out of sympathy. But with the rarest opportunities for
giving his country a new birth of righteousness and liberty, that has
ever come to any man, he has done nothing. He has not justified the
people of America in conferring their highest honor upon him. But as
Aeschines[11] said, when he debated the question whether Demosthenes
should be crowned, he has left his country to be judged by its youth
because of the man who has received its greatest honor. "When a man

votes against what is noble and just," said Aeschines, "and then comes home to teach his son, the boy will very properly say, 'Your lesson is impertinent and a bore.'" Hence, what is courage without a cause; what is strenuosity without an ideal?

The temptation considered symbolically alone is the most searching analysis of every man's experience in the realm of literature. The Son of Man was a hungered and the tempter said, "If thou be the son of God command that these stones be made bread." Again, the Son of Man was tempted to use his power for a vain and foolish purpose, and by such use to place himself upon the level of mountebanks and magicians. Finally, empire over the world was offered him, if he would worship the principle of evil. In the resistance of these temptations is symbolized honorable poverty, dignified purpose and renunciation of political power rather than to sacrifice those principles without which political power is a curse.

One of Mr. Roosevelt's apologists has said that he compromised with his ideals in order to get power to carry some of them into effect but this never has and never can be done. The man who thus sophisticates with his own mind has surrendered his power. He has fallen at the feet of evil in order to possess a kingdom; and he leaves behind him when he enters into possession, the only power by which he could serve the kingdom or glorify himself. If Mr. Roosevelt's pretensions to ideals in his earlier years may be considered seriously it only remains to say that in various books he stood against the flagrant evil of a protective tariff; that he denounced imperialism, that is, the acquisition of distant and heterogeneous territory by force; and that he never lost an opportunity to inveigh against the spoils system in the government service. When he capitulated upon these principles to get office, he had nothing left with which to seriously employ his courage or his strenuosity. It was a long step from the advocacy of expansion by the addition of sovereign and contiguous states to the advocacy of subjugating a whole nation at the farther side of the globe. Yet when Mr. Roosevelt parted with his principles he did not abandon his intemperate hatreds. "Cowardly shrinking from duty," as applied to the policy expressed in the democratic platform of 1900 contains a good deal of sound and fury, but it signified nothing unless it drowned out the small voice in himself that appealed to his own utterances in favor of liberty in his biography of Thomas H. Benton.[12] Hence did he compromise with his principles in order to get into power to do good? When his country hesitated before taking the plunge into national animalism he was present to denounce those as cowards who tried to restrain it. He became the loudest exponent of swaggering militarism. He has given repeated expression to that vulgarity which arrayed in garish colors sets up to despise the day of high thinking and noble simplicity. The strenuous life consists in hearty feeding, mighty hunting, desperate climbing, and daily exercise upon the mat or with the gloves. Yet he is the cynosure of vast numbers of the wealth and fashion of the country, who find in him a proud and distinguished interpreter of the cult of exuberant animalism. The slaughter of the ostrich, the rhinoceros and the elephant in the Roman amphitheater with the bow and arrow held by the skillful hand of the imperial hunter is out-done by the pursuit of bears and mountain lions with modern weapons before an audience of millions. The daily press with its pictorial facilities has increased the spectators and multiplied the marvels. Scattered through the various strata of society Mr. Roosevelt has found sincere admirers. A military spirit, which slumbers in the breast of the man below who loves to fight and the man above who loves to see a fight, has leaped forward to claim Mr. Roosevelt as something typically American. Thus he is not without friends in any of the classes drawn according to the common standards. His election to the vice-presidency elated an exponent of the culture of the land, so that even beneath the shades of classicism he is not wholly proscribed. Churchmen, who, with a vague unrest, are ever reaching out for new realms of activity, and keener realizations of power, take him as the possible precursor of some destiny toward which they have hitherto drifted unconsciously. With his friends it is useless to point out that he has discarded the institutions of his country and broken its ideals. For principles of peace and good will toward all nations he has substituted military rivalry. He has transported hither the spirit of doubt which obtains among European nations whose proximity to each other and whose traditional jealousies have kept up a wearisome watchfulness.

Many things, which by reason of what Washington called our peculiar situation, are alien to us he has helped to cultivate among us. One hundred years have not sufficed to make these growths of old world conditions indigenous to this soil. We are yet what we were in Washington's day, a nation set apart from the quarrels of kings; and it is strange indeed if some dream of destiny which would have discredited Louis Napoleon, shall carry us far away from that simple code which is logically evolved from our natural situation.

Mr. Roosevelt well illustrates the principle that the decay of liberty corrupts one of the noblest arts. What can account for his speeches in which the American people are advised to carry a big stick in which policemen are praised for their swift running, and in which mighty valor, mighty deeds, great daring and such subjects are the changes which are rung? Sober people listen in amazement to these singular strains, well understanding that they cannot help but vitiate popular sentiment at home and produce anxiety and hatred abroad. A man who carries a stick or a pistol will more likely be attacked than the man who does not go armed. For the arming of one's self is the result of a feeling of hate and the very fact that he is armed makes him dangerous to those who are not. The impulse of self-preservation prompts the removal of the danger. These things are as true of nations as of men. To keep the country upon the edge of war because of some fancied contingency, and to depart into a path of danger for the sole purpose of greatly daring and bravely facing whatever peril may come, involve the overthrow of all this country has hitherto stood for, and that through a spirit of boyish bravado. Nothing more absurd has ever occurred in the history of any nation. To speak of mere form, there is a marked rhetorical difference between Mr. McKinley's apostrophic question "who will haul down the flag" and Mr. Roosevelt's crude declaration that "the flag will stay put." As an orator Mr. Roosevelt has nothing to say and says it as poorly as possible.

Court etiquette at the White House is only a reflex of more fundamental changes. The transformation of that historic building into a palace; the ruthless removal and storage of cherished pictures and furniture; the galloping of cavalry through the streets of the capital attending upon officials or embassies; the designation of Mr. Roosevelt as "the presence" which is now done in the reports of the social functions of the White House; a rigid system of caste; a policy of militarism, inquisition and espionage in the executive department of the government are also significant things which cannot be overlooked.

It goes without saying that Mr. Roosevelt has never shown any regard for constitutional liberty; and that he seems to have little understanding of the real forces of civilization. Those who will attend to the lesson may learn that nothing can ever come of observing the little virtues while the weightier matters of the law are neglected. The lack of great principles and those firmly adhered to can never be compensated by intentions, however good or by private virtues however admirable. Sanguine spirits comfort themselves with the thought that if Mr. Roosevelt is given power on his own account that he will not carry out another's policy but will consider himself free to pursue one of his own. If he was looking for an immortality as glorious as any known to history he could achieve it by giving this country a new birth of freedom. The republic is groaning under the weight of sin. Its conscience is tormented with a sense of awful guilt, with a knowledge of duty forsaken and ideals discarded and shattered. Millions of men who love the republic and who took no part in its iniquities look forward with passionate hearts to a return, of liberty. If Mr. Roosevelt should be able to withdraw our control from the Philippines and assist these people in establishing a republic he would justly stand for all times as the most colossal figure of the twentieth century. Here is a field for his courage and his strenuosity. Here is an opportunity which a truly wise man would not pass over. But it is not likely that he will fulfill any such expectations. He abandoned his ideals to get office. He will reassure the master forces of his party in order to be elected president. He will go into office with the chains which are the price of moral surrender. He is too vain, too infatuated with the sophistry of privilege and glory to do differently in the future from what he has done in the past. He has robed the office of president, and the government itself, so far as under his control, in the splendor and pomp of monarchy. This is apparel which speaks the man. As he called Jefferson a "shifty doctrinaire," and Polk[13] a man of "monumental littleness" he cannot complain if history shall write him down as one whose inordinate egotism and prostituted principles endangered for a time the hopes of mankind.

Notes

1. Johann Wolfgang von Goethe (1749–1832) was a German author with a widespread influence on German literature and culture. See Brent O. Peterson and Martha B. Helfer, "Why Goethe Needs German Studies and Why German Studies Needs Goethe," *German Studies Review* 35, no. 3 (2012): 470-474.

2. Johann Christoph Friedrich von Schiller (1759–1805) was a German playwright; *"William Tell"* (1804) was one of his most popular works. The main theme of the story of William Tell is fighting for freedom and standing up against tyranny. See Roger E. Mitchell and Joyce P. Mitchell, "Schiller's William Tell: A Folkloristic Perspective," *Journal of American Folklore* 83, no. 327 (1970): 44–52.

3. A hat with a brim that hangs down, commonly worn as part of a military uniform. *Webster's Practical Dictionary*, s.v. "slouch hat."

4. "Lead a pug dog" is in reference to one of the many animals the Roosevelts had during his presidency. His wife, Alice, was gifted a pug from the last empress of China during a visit. "The Roosevelt Pets," National Park Service, accessed February 28, 2022, https://www.nps.gov/thrb/learn/historyculture/the-roosevelt-pets.htm.

5. Masters, here, likely refers to Kaiser Wilhelm II (1859–1941), who was emperor of Germany (1888–1918) when this essay was written.

6. Rudyard Kipling (1865–1936), poet, was a voice for imperialist views during the late nineteenth century. See Gordon Williams, "Rudyard Kipling and His Critics," *Australian Quarterly* 8, no. 30 (1936): 65–70.

7. A Rudyard Kipling poem, published in 1897, that controversially promoted imperialism while using the language of a traditional jeremiad. See A. W. Yeats, "The Genesis of 'The Recessional,'" *University of Texas Studies in English* 31 (1952): 97–108.

8. Commodus (161-192) was a Roman emperor who ruled jointly with his father, Marcus Aurelius, from 176-180, and sole emperor of Rome from 180-192. His reign is remembered as one of increasing cruelty in the years before his assassination.

9. The Philippine American conflict, which lasted from 1899 to 1902, began during American occupation of the Philippine Islands following the end of the Spanish-American War. In 1901, Theodore Roosevelt (1858–1919) became president of the United States after William McKinley's (1843–1901) assassination. See David J. Silbey, *A War of Frontier and Empire: The Philippine-American War, 1899–1902* (New York: Hill and Wang, 2007).

10. Theodore Roosevelt made this phrase—originally derived from the West African proverb "Speak softly and carry a big stick; you will go far"—famous

as a characterization of his foreign policy. See Edward P. Kohn, "A Benign Big Stick: Theodore Roosevelt and Global Policing", review of *Theodore Roosevelt and World Order: Police Power in International Relations*, by James R. Holmes, *Journal of the Gilded Age and Progressive Era* 7, no. 1 (2008): 132–35.

11. Aeschines (389–314 BCE) was an Athenian politician and orator.

12. Thomas Hart Benton (1782–1858) was a Democrat from Missouri.

13. James K. Polk (1795–1849), president of the United States (1845–49), Democrat. Polk was president during the Mexican-American War (1846–48), where the United States acquired much of the modern American Southwest in the Treaty of Guadalupe Hidalgo.

John Marshall

A **MONG** the signs of the times which bode ill for the purity of republican principles is the much-vaunted plan of celebrating the memory of John Marshall. This analysis of the movement is indisputably true—namely, if its patrons were devoted to the rights of men instead of the powers of government, if they were stirred by the principles of liberty instead of the glory of the state they would propose to celebrate by proper memorials the achievements and sacrifices of some one of the many men who pledged life and sacred honor in the cause of American liberty and who sought to bequeath it to posterity when it was attained.

Those thinkers who place the state on a higher plane than men are usually engaged in defending unequal rights. When rights are unequal the state must be strong enough not only to make them so, but to keep them so. It ought to be a plain truth to everyone that the only justification for government is the preservation of equal rights. Men are endowed with the love of liberty and with an intuitive sense of its axiomatic truth. And when the constitution was adopted its climacteric end was stated in the preamble to be the preservation of liberty to ourselves and our posterity. But in proportion as the government becomes strong men become weak. In proportion as the functions of government are multiplied individual liberty is decreased. Therefore as we must have both government and liberty what powers shall the government have?

There is but one answer to this question. When the government is strong enough to protect each man in the enjoyment of equal freedom it has attained the full measure of legitimate power.

One of the envious shadows that has fallen from the black cockade[1] of federalism is the forgery of history against those who believed in liberty, and who, although favorable to the creation of a nation, endeavored to preserve individual freedom. Jefferson, who understood the science of government better than any American, has been so calumniated by monarchial writers that nothing has saved the purity of his fame except the voluminous documents and letters which he left behind him, making the attempt to belie his principles impossible to those who can investigate the question with care. And yet a vulgar impression exists that Jefferson was inimical to the constitution. By a skillful process of innuendo and sophistication his principles have been intermixed with the doctrines of Calhoun[2] and the attempt has been made to place them in a fostering relation to anarchy and rebellion. By a like process Marshall is made to stand as the great friend of government and the effectual exponent of law and order. The minds of the American people have been greatly abused by these fictions, which are the creation of those monarchists who, as the miners and sappers of the constitution, in favor of themselves have thus falsely appealed to the Anglo-Saxon love of sound government.

The absurd eulogium which is habitually passed upon Marshall is that he made a nation of the United States. A franker avowal, but with the same meaning, is that he strengthened the government; while latterly the whole significance of these utterances is unmasked in the bold acclaim that he was the first man to take up the march of the constitution. He is praised as having written implied powers in the constitution, and history has been manipulated to establish a sequence between his decision in McCulloch vs. Maryland and the battle of Gettysburg.[3] But, while a certain school of political thought has insisted that the victory at Gettysburg was the approval of arms of that decision and that implied powers may be written into the constitution whenever desirable, and that even the constitution may be disregarded in the interests of government, they should not forget that the battle of Bunker hill [sic] decided that there shall be neither kings nor monarchists anywhere in America.

Then, with all due respect to the private character, public services and known abilities of John Marshall, why apotheosize his memory at this time? In this year the declaration of independence is characterized as a revolutionary pronunciamento[4] incapable of syllogistic proof. The constitution is ignored. A president is governing millions of people outside of the constitution, admits that he is doing so and says that it is proper to do so. Is it not an additional comment of the same purport upon the spirit of the time to flood the country with panegyrics[5] upon the great expositor of implied powers? If these things find warrant in the principles of Jefferson, Story,[6] Adams, Madison, Randolph[7] or Paine and not in Marshall, why not celebrate one of the former? For, rightfully considered, Marshall occupies a mere secondary place among the great men of this country.

Hamilton possessed a more daring and original genius, but a cabinet report on a national bank lacks the force of a supreme court decision finding its charter to be constitutional. Madison excelled him in learning, but Madison was in favor of a constitutional march only by a constitutional amendment. Franklin's mind was more versatile, but Franklin, though dissatisfied with the monarchial faults of the constitution, acquiesced in it when the majority favored it for the good it contained and the peace of the country. Jefferson towered above him in all that goes to constitute the statesman, humanity, vast scholarship, deep insight and grasp of principles, but Jefferson was a friend to the constitution, not as those who became its enemies when they could not use it. Not even Marshall's warmest admirers claim he was a man of more than mediocre juridical learning. As a judge he was inferior to many of his associates in scholarship, while his successor, Taney, was a more brilliant example of judicial genius.[8]

But after all such discriminations as these how does the judicial office, however capably filled, compare with those efforts of ampler genius which uplift and enlighten the race of men? Marshall possessed that cast of mind which would have won him success in Scottish metaphysics exemplified by the writings of Dugald Stewart.[9] But as Taine[10] has well said that the English language has known no metaphysician, Marshall's mental cast was of that inferior order which gave him mere ingenuity in sophisticating legal questions to a preconceived idea. His habit of covering the whole field of discussion in long obiter dicta[11] when the case turned upon a point of jurisdiction was not only disingenuous, but has actually corrupted all federal decisions to this day with the same defect.

In Marbury vs. Madison, where the sole question was whether the supreme court had jurisdiction of the writ of mandamus[12] under the constitution to compel Madison to deliver certain commissions, Marshall treated the whole question, finding that the commissions were valid, although never delivered, and then decided at last that the court had no jurisdiction to do anything. It was this course in the Dred Scott[13] case in which the court discussed every political and historical aspect of slavery, only to hold that Dred Scott was a slave and could not sue in the United States courts, that rocked the republic to its foundations and caused Lincoln to say that the people are masters of both congress and courts, not to overthrow the constitution, but to overthrow those who pervert the constitution.

But it is because Marshall's career subserves a desire as old as the declaration of independence that his memory is nourished to the neglect of many great men who stood opposed to his principles. From documents and diaries, from historical evidence not to be doubted, there has existed in this country from the close of the revolutionary war a powerful party fortified by intelligence, respectability and wealth and sleepless in its efforts to monarchize the republic. It is not pretended that this party desired a king. But a king is not necessary to monarchial success.

Where the elective principle is wormed out, where the superior branch of the legislature is independent of the people, where the executive is independent of the people and the judiciary sits above impeachment, where the constitution, whose very object was to prevent by its limitations a perversion of the republic, is treated with contempt or amended by judicial construction and not by the people, as it provides, and where these functionaries of government legislate upon the theories of inequality before the law, in that manner building up a powerful aristocracy, which uses its force to continue these policies, there the monarchial principle has been established. It was for these things by temperament, by conduct and by judicial decision that Marshall stood.

If the declaration of independence was a mere revolutionary manifesto then it only accomplished our emancipation from the government of Great Britain. But if it was a statement of political truths applicable to all men at all times then it divorced the American people forever from all monarchial principles. It became the soul of the constitution, just as it animated the thought of Madison and the great leaders of liberty in the constitutional convention. But the pure intent of the father was corrupted by the illegitimate reasoning of Hamilton, just as amid the swell of a triumphant chorus one discordant blast may destroy the entire harmony. And when he had once introduced the voice of monarchy into the theme the best that could be done with the unfitting tone was to temper it as much as possible to the main key. The absurd electoral college was one of the results of this endeavor. The venerable Franklin just before signing the constitution sadly declared that it was perhaps the best constitution that could be evolved from the materials at hand and that the government could only, like all others before it, end in despotism.

When it is remembered that Hamilton frankly avowed monarchial principles and that in numerous letters and declarations he purposed under the guise of implied powers to create a government different from that created by the constitution, and when it is remembered in this connection that Marshall as a judge completed his work by validating Hamiltonian legislation, the component parts of a scheme to monarchize the republic are brought to view. It was by the funded debt, the tariff, the United States bank and internal improvements that the constitution was to be destroyed in its own name. For when it was objected that the constitution should not have a permanent debt Hamilton illogically replied that the people should not repudiate the price of liberty. When it was urged that the constitution did not warrant the exaction of toll for the benefit of merchants Hamilton with accustomed sophistry replied that American labor must be protected. When the United States bank was opposed as unconstitutional Hamilton pointed to the war clause in the constitution and appealed to the war spirit of the people. When internal improvements were resisted on the ground that they were unconstitutional and furnished the means of general corruption Hamilton asked if the people did not desire to foster domestic commerce by building passable highways through the country. Thus while arguing beside the point with the people he conveyed to his followers the real purpose of these things— namely, the march of the constitution toward an aristocracy.

It is impossible within any reasonable space to picture the sufferings of men through the long ages at the hands of tyrants or to show that beyond the boundaries of a republic lies the domain of monarchy where the sun of truth does not shine, because monarchy will not suffer itself to be explored, knowing that it is defended by the monsters of force and fraud. Language, therefore, is weak when an attempt is made to characterize the Hamiltonian plot against the great republic which came into being after centuries of struggle, endowed with the pacific wisdom of the greatest men of Greece and Rome and England. Who can sufficiently condemn any plot designed to turn the republic back into the hateful paths of despotism? Centuries hence, when perhaps the democratic principles shall have been put beyond assault by bloody revolutions and this undergrowth of dialectics concerning implied powers shall have been burned up in the fierce heat of outraged humanity, men will wonder at the darkness with which the evil genius of Hamilton and Marshall obscured the light of heaven.

It is conceded by Marshall's warmest admirers that his reasoning in McCulloch vs. Maryland was adopted from Hamilton's report on a national bank. The latter is at once the most patent as well as the most artful piece of unreason in the language. Most patent because no man of candid sense can fail to perceive its fallacies. It is most artful because almost impossible of disproof to any man whose intuitive sense of logic does not grasp its refutation in its own terms. It is comparable to nothing in any language more than to the puerile sophistry of Plato. Yet history has been fabricated and criticisms written to exalt this sinister document. It is supposed to add to the celebrity of Marshall that he followed its irrational windings in adjudging the charter of the United States bank to be constitutional.

As the charter violated the laws of mortmain and alienage, of descent and distribution, there was in these things sufficient reason for invalidating it.[14] As it created a monopoly and therefore invaded the principles of liberty, the bank had no place in the republic. As it was invested with powers paramount to the states, it trespassed upon that sovereignty of the states which is limited only by the sovereignty of the general government. As the bank was an economic heresy, it was not a proper means of carrying into effect any enumerated power of congress. As the constitutional convention had voted down a proposition to authorize congress to open canals and to incorporate companies, because congress would then be empowered to incorporate a bank, Hamilton's report asserted an implied power in congress to do that which the convention had expressly refused to confer upon congress.

Therefore, as the constitutional debates might be ignored upon the principle that all intents became merged in the constitution, although Marshall himself frequently quoted the Federalist[15] in deciding questions, still, as the constitution was silent on the power to incorporate a bank, a trading company or any other corporation, it became incumbent upon Hamilton to establish a relation between a bank and one of the enumerated powers as being "necessary and proper" to effectuate it. Here refinement reached the level of medieval metaphysics. Hamilton asserted that "necessary" meant needful, requisite, incidental, useful or conducive to. On the other hand, Jefferson contended that necessary means constituted those "without which the grant of power would be nugatory."

It is apparent that many things might be useful to the execution of some enumerated power or in some manner incidental to its execution without bearing that legitimate relation to it which in its absence would render the enumerated power incapable of execution. Then Hamilton sought to bring the creation of the bank within the implied powers of congress. He argued that it related to the collection of taxes, because it increased the circulating medium, and, therefore, facilitated the payment of taxes. But as congress is only empowered to lay taxes and pay debts, the bill to create the bank laid no tax and paid no debt. He argued that it related to the power of borrowing money. But the bill neither borrowed money nor provided for borrowing money. He argued that it related to the regulation of commerce between the several states. But the bill did not regulate commerce, but only created a subject of commerce in its paper money, just as any producer of wealth creates subjects of commerce, but does not regulate them by such production. Instances of the argument need not further be multiplied to demonstrate the fallacy of Hamilton's report.

Hamilton then entertained the avowed project of monarchizing the republic and warded off attacks upon him by the demagogic plea that the sovereignty of the nation must not be crippled. No one ever entertained that purpose. But the constitution was adopted by the fathers and defended by Jefferson for the purpose of crippling the imperialistic attempts of that body of thinkers who believed in monarchial government.

Among candid men it can never be debatable that in this government, conceived in liberty and dedicated to the proposition that all men are created equal, its constitution impliedly warrants the erection of a monopoly. Nor can it be debatable that a government so founded by force of its constitution permits any legislation as necessary to carry into effect some express power which in its intent and practice constitutes pure aggression. It was never intended that implied powers should be written into the constitution in favor of the monarchial principle of special privilege and that it should be strictly construed against the republican principle of liberty.

Marshall well knew that the United States bank, by virtue of the special privileges granted it, absolutely dominated the financial system of the land, and that it had the power to destroy every moneyed institution in the country and to reduce to beggary almost countless thousands of people. How could legislation creating such an institution be held as constitutional when not expressly provided for in the constitution and asserted to be impliedly provided for in a piece of far-fetched and fantastic unreason? In the absence of Marshall's positive declarations, his bank decision is sufficient to stamp him as an enemy of republican principles.

Upon this foundation the fame of Marshall rests. He was not a friend to the constitution or to republican institutions. And as showing that his decision in the bank case was the result of a temperamental leaning in favor of a monarchial system and that it did not result from the logic of discussion the opinion of Allan B. Magruder,[16] Marshall's panegyrist, is in point. "He," wrote Magruder, "made federalist law in nine cases out of ten and made it in strong, shapely fashion. A republican judge, however, would have brought about a very different result, which as we believe would have been vastly less serviceable to the people, but of which the workmanship in a strictly professional and technical view might have been equally correct."

A vulgar view of the matter created by federalistic sophistry is that Marshall's decisions somehow armed the northern arms to deal the death blow to anarchy, Calhounism and strict constructionism, supposed to have been championed by Jefferson. Herein these irreconcilable things have been falsely confused. The civil war decided nothing new whatever. It merely destroyed by force the doctrines of Calhoun that the constitution itself provides by implication for the peaceable dissolution of the union. But it did not decide that the constitution by virtue of its implied powers provides for the erection of monarchy upon its ruins. And yet how have the Hamiltonians manipulated the effects of the war and distorted its meaning if not to cry out that all constitutional questions were laid at rest by the war? They declare that strict construction, a mere federalistic fiction, was shot to death at Gettysburg, as if that gave them the warrant to write such implied powers into the riddled constitution as they desire, or even to ignore it for the purpose of throwing off its crippling limitations in order that the United States may be as powerful as the monarchies of the old world.

Thus have Hamiltonism and Marshallism conducted the republic to imperialism. However pure Marshall's private character may have been, however exalted his abilities or however patriotic his course in the revolutionary war his career stands for evil in the republic if his influence leads to the overthrow of the constitution or can be employed to that end. It was not confidence in man but in distrust of human nature, that the constitution was adopted reserving to the states or the people all powers not delegated to the United States. "To take a single step beyond the boundaries thus specially drawn around the powers of congress is to take possession of a boundless field of power no longer susceptible of any definition."[17] The doctrine of implied powers as construed by Marshall is a flat contradiction of the very intent of the constitution and thus turns into futility the declaration of independence. The blood of those who fell at Lexington and Concord cries out against their evil activity.

To what beginning do the American people look for their government? To the exalted thought of revolutionary demigods and to the
consent of that bold people who adopted a written constitution by
popular voice. To what beginning do the English people look for their
government? To the force of William the Conqueror,[18] who subdued
and despoiled them by the sword and ruled them in contempt of their
choice. Why confuse these two systems? Why exalt those who avowedly
sought to pervert the republic and cast the shadow of unmerited shame
upon those who founded the only republic that ever existed? The experiment is in the hands of the American people. They may destroy the
republic, but they cannot obliterate the principles of Jefferson and the
declaration of independence. If in the evolution of the world's history
this republic was not destined to be perpetuated the truths upon which
it was founded will nevertheless survive all the shocks of time and will
become the corner stones of some perfect fabric ages hence, so that a
government of the people shall indeed not perish from the earth.

Notes

1. "A rosette or knot of ribbons, etc., on the hat." Cockades were decorative and
commonly worn as a symbol of political allegiance to a specific group. *Webster's
Practical Dictionary*, s.v. "cockade."

2. John C. Calhoun (1782–1850), senator, secretary of state, secretary of war,
and vice president of the United States, was a staunch supporter of slavery
and states' rights. See Robert Elder, *Calhoun: American Heretic* (New York: Basic
Books, 2021).

3. *McCulloch v. Maryland* (1819) was a U.S. Supreme Court case overseen by John
Marshall (1755-1835), chief justice of the Supreme Court. In this case, the State
of Maryland levied a tax on the National Bank, which McCulloch, a cashier at
the bank, refused to pay. The Supreme Court ruled unanimously in favor of
McCulloch and the Second Bank, thus strengthening the power of the legislative branch by defending its ability to charter a bank, giving more credence to
implied powers in the Constitution. See Clyde Ray, "John Marshall, *McCulloch
v. Maryland*, and the Concept of Constitutional Sovereignty," *Perspectives on
Political Science* 47, no. 2 (April–June 2018): 65–77.

4. A nineteenth-century Spanish phrase meaning a manifesto, formal announce-
ment, or declaration, usually in connection with a coup d'état, revolution, or
rebellion. *Webster's Practical Dictionary*, s.v. "pronunciamento."

5. "An oration in praise of some person or achievement." *Webster's Practical Dictionary*, s.v. "panegyric."

6. Joseph Story (1779–1845) was an associate justice of the Supreme Court who frequently concurred with John Marshall during Marshall's tenure as chief justice, particularly in cases that expanded federal power. See R. Kent Newmyer, *Supreme Court Justice Joseph Story: Statesman of the Old Republic* (Chapel Hill: University of North Carolina Press, 2004).

7. Edmund Randolph (1753-1813) was a Virginian delegate to the Constitutional Convention and, later served as secretary of state and attorney general during George Washington's presidency.

8. Roger B. Taney (1777–1864), Supreme Court chief justice (1836–64). Taney was chief justice during the *Dred Scott v. Sanford* case (1857), where he wrote the opinion for the majority. Masters is likely celebrating Taney's legacy in this section for decisions like *Charles River Bridge v. Warren Bridge* (1837), where the court ruled that Massachusetts could not charter monopoly power to favored businesses. Likewise, in *Briscoe v. Commonwealth Bank of Kentucky* (1837), Taney and the court supported the issuing of bank notes by state-chartered banks, thereby affirming Andrew Jackson's distribution of public deposits from the National Bank to state banks. Taney was himself secretary of the Treasury when Jackson implemented this policy. These pro–states' rights decisions align with Masters's Populist ideology.

9. Dugald Stewart (1753–1828) was a Scottish philosopher during the Enlightenment who taught mathematics and moral philosophy at the University of Edinburgh.

10. Hippolyte-Adolphe Taine (1828–93) was a French historian and critic. See Leo Weinstein, *Hippolyte Taine* (New York: Twayne, 1972).

11. "Obiter dicta" is a Latin phrase meaning "that which is said in passing." It is commonly used in law to refer to pieces of judicial opinion that are included with the rest of the opinion but not related directly to the opinion.

12. A legal term for "court order." In the case *Marbury v. Madison* (1803), the Supreme Court determined whether the Court had the constitutional authority to compel Secretary of State Madison to deliver notification of the judicial appointment of William Marbury to Justice of the Peace of Washington, D.C. Marbury was one of the "midnight" appointments of President John Adams under the Judiciary Act of 1801, where the outgoing Federalist administration sought to fill federal court positions with political allies before the inauguration of Thomas Jefferson. The Supreme Court decided that Madison had an obligation to deliver Marbury's commission, but did not issue a writ of mandamus to the Secretary of State, determining that the Judiciary Act of 1789, which granted the Supreme Court the right to issue writs of mandamus in these circumstances was, itself, unconstitutional. Subsequently, Madison

never issued a commission for Marbury's appointment to Justice of the Peace of Washington, D.C.

13. In the notorious *Dred Scott* case, Chief Justice Roger Taney returned Dred Scott to servitude with the argument that enslaved people maintained their enslaved status while residing in states where slavery was illegal. Taney also argued that the Constitution was intended only for white citizens and that Scott's claim had no standing before the court.

14. Masters here echoes Jefferson's argument against Hamilton's proposal for the chartering of the National Bank: "The bill for establishing a National Bank undertakes, among other things 1. to form the subscribers into a Corporation. 2. to enable them, in their corporate capacities to receive grants of land; and so far is against the laws of Mortmain [,] though the constitution controuls [sic] the laws of Mortmain so far as to permit Congress itself to hold lands for certain purposes, yet not so far as to permit them to communicate a similar right to other corporate bodies. 3. to make aliens ubscribers capable of holding lands, & so far is against the laws of Alienage. 4. to transmit these lands, on the death of a proprietor, to a certain line of successors: & so far changes the course of Descents." See "To George Washington from Thomas Jefferson, 15, February 1791," *Founders Online*, https://founders.archives.gov/documents/Washington/05-07-02-0207 [accessed 14, January 2022].

15. The Federalist Papers were a series of eighty-five essays and papers written by Alexander Hamilton (1755 or 1757-1804), John Jay (1745-1829), and James Madison (1751-1836), published between 1787 and 1788. They were issued anonymously under the pen name "Publius" in a variety of newspapers. Their goal was to convince readers to support ratification of the then-pending Constitution.

16. Allan B. Magruder (1775–1822) was a Democratic-Republican representative from Louisiana who was elected to the U.S. Senate in 1812 and served a single term.

17. Masters here again quotes Jefferson's correspondence to Washington over concern with the precedent set by the creation of the National Bank.

18. William the Conqueror (c. 1028–87) was a Norman-French duke who took control of England in 1066 after the Battle of Hastings. See David Bates, *William the Conqueror* (New Haven: Yale University Press, 2016).

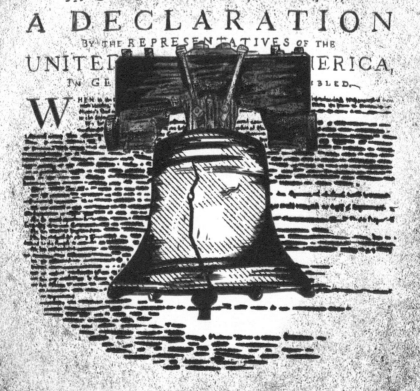

Thomas Jefferson

JEFFERSON'S birthday in these days is not generally celebrated at the banquet board. His character lacked the militant element which lends itself to the paganistic rites of the feast, the toast, and the high-sounding eulogium. He won no battles, he conquered no visible foe, he captured no concrete strongholds. His life was intellectual and peaceful. His mind was engaged with the sciences, with historical studies, with the practical arts, with music, with polite literature and with a new form of statesmanship. He had sworn eternal hostility against every form of tyranny over the mind of man. The warfare which he waged was in the domain of mind. It was against injustice, special privilege, ignorance and bigotry.[1] These were the foes whose citadels he reduced and whose armies he subdued. Do such victories appeal to the heavy imagination of commercialism? Moreover, Jefferson is memorialized on the 4th of July, which as a national holiday really engages itself with honoring the work of this man. Who else in American history has such universal tribute paid him?

Latterly also the root and branch of despotism have flourished to some extent in this land and a systematic effort is apparent to find some other character prophetic of the day and sympathetic with its temporary movement. Jefferson will not suffer to any great extent by this conspiracy. He will come into his own in due season. He is the genius of this republic and of the republican system and his course was not accomplished to be supplanted by some secondary influence. The real logic of history is not that way. He is to statesmanship what Luther was to the reformation and Newton to science. And he shares with them to some extent their disadvantage of after-dinner talk. But, on the other hand, who else furnishes a better theme for oratory as that art should be practiced? Here was a hundred handed man. He was a great lawyer, he was a scientist, a musician, a scholar, an inventor, a writer and a statesman. Like Goethe, he studied everything and tried everything. He was mediocre in nothing that he attempted. He had observed the proprieties of life. Scandal never touched his name. Party rancor failed to impeach his motives. He was just. He was generous. He was devoted to liberty and truth. There was no humbug in him. He developed no mysticism of a flag with which to enslave the minds of his fellows. He put government in the sunlight, where its workings could be seen. He was therefore hated by those who wanted to perpetuate the superstitions of the past that the administration of public affairs is a mysterious agency not to be analyzed but to be feared and worshiped. His comprehensive mind grasped the spirit of the day. If he discovered no political principles he stated those already known in such language that they have become the very elements of thought. He is the most conspicuous success in history in the application of great principles to practical affairs. He carved out the sphere of the state. He defined the rights of the citizen in the state. He furnished every president after him, including Lincoln, with a policy and a reason for the policy. There is no system in opposition to his which is avowed and denied. Even imperialism is justified under the pretense of giving the Filipinos liberty. What greater tribute can his enemies pay him when they fear to do evil, except in the name of Jefferson? They admit his power in the land when they call the Philippine aggression the same thing as the Louisiana purchase.

What man at 33 years of age has contributed to civilization in any form such a motive power as the declaration of independence? This was an inspirational stroke which fitted into the time; in fact, we cannot conceive of the world without it. It interprets the new epoch. It is a charter of liberty beside which magna charta and the instrument of government are as dull as a declaration for slander. Who else had so elevated his mind and humanized his heart that he could have written it? It stated fundamental truths, but in such language that they armed revolution, fired the conscience of the people and raised the hopes of a discouraged land. It contains within itself all the aspiration, all the justice and all the beneficence of the human heart. It is intelligible, compact, incapable of being misunderstood or sophisticated. It means the same thing to all men. It is all-inclusive. It is a perfect repository of political truth and philosophy. It defies the insolence of monarchy and grinds to powder the absurd pretension of divine right. It takes the angry assaults of selfish expediency and special privilege without hurt. It is unchangeable in its appeal and is heard with rapture by millions once a year in every city and hamlet in the land.[2] It challenges refutation and where proscribed is not answered. It is feared by those whose power rests upon fraud or force. It conquers, but does not wound; it leaves no sting after the mind has been subdued; it wins its way through a spirit of amity and reason. Such is the declaration of independence, defeated on many battlefields since it was promulgated. But it has never been overthrown in the forum, in the realm of reason. All victories of force are barren which are not crowned by truth and justice. It were better that they were never won.

The civil war brought to the front a form of man not intended to flourish in this country. He is that banal demagogue who wishes to clothe in the sacredness of government whatever a paramount political party chooses to do. He takes occasion to denounce protest against usurpation as rebellion and treason. He conjures with the words "sovereignty" and "the flag." At the banquet board, where his resounding hypocrisies are launched, he starts with Thomas Jefferson as the author of secession and the proximate cause of the civil war. His peroration invests with the halo of divine dispensation the Philippine despotism. The critics of that despotism are branded as traitors. They are held responsible for the death of our boys in the islands. The honor of the army engages his swelling wrath and he sits down amidst the applause of those who have more respect for the rules of golf than they have for the constitution of the United States. These are the scenes now enacted in a republic where, properly speaking, there is no such thing as the honor of the army or the act of any administration, even if crystallized into law, which forbids condemnation, oral and written, and proper effort to restore the government to liberty and law. There are many millions of men in this country who care nothing about the army and who are perfectly sure that it can have no honor while it is engaged in subjugation. They will not defer in their opinions to those who profit by that subjugation, and who would wreck the country before they would part with their anticonstitutional protective tariff.[3] If what they say of Jefferson is true, how shall these self-appointed patriots complain? Who will explain the difference between breaking up the union by secession and destroying the union by annihilating the organic law which created the union and holds it together?

Jefferson in the Kentucky resolutions,[4] in which the seeds of secession were said to be, attacked the palpable infractions of the constitution made by the tariff laws, the United States bank act[5] and the alien and sedition acts.[6] The resolutions were particularly called out by the alien and sedition acts. And a question as old as government and not yet settled arose by their passage, namely, Must people submit to tyranny to escape the charge of treason preferred by the temporary administers of the government? Human nature will take care of this problem. Men are not so cowardly or so weak that they will part with their liberties in order to earn the commendation of being loyal. The Kentucky resolutions were the prompt reaction against the studied attempts of the anticonstitutionalists to destroy the republic, but they do not advocate secession. They do not go as far as the enemies of Jefferson wish they did. Jefferson was not a secessionist. His letters to John Taylor,[7] Richard Rush[8] and Elbridge Gary[9] belie the charge that he advocated secession. The argument which Lincoln used with great effect, that secession would haunt secession and ultimately break up any group of seceded states, was Jefferson's. He applied it to the case of New England, which contemplated secession on account of the war of 1812.

It was at a dinner given in honor of Jefferson's birthday, April 13, 1830, that his name was first coupled with secession and that in a vague and somewhat subtle form. For President Jackson on that occasion responded to the toast "Our Federal Union: It Must Be Preserved." This would have settled the character of the dinner except for the toast of Mr. Calhoun, who said: "The union, next to our liberty the most dear; may we all remember that it can only be preserved by respecting the rights of the states and distributing equally the benefits and burthens of the union." These remarks were coupled with the circumstances of the day in the south looking toward disunion which served to identify Jefferson's name with the doctrine of the right of a state to withdraw from the union.

But the Kentucky resolutions advocated nullification, not secession. They assert the right of a state to stay in the union and nullify a law of the general government. "Where powers are assumed which have not been delegated a nullification is the rightful remedy." This is the language of the resolutions. The word secession nowhere appears in them. The right to nullify is based upon the assumption that an unconstitutional law is null and void and no law. That an unconstitutional law is no law is the judgment of the supreme court to this day. That court holds now that such a law may be disregarded by everyone. If so, a state could disregard it. But the resolutions go beyond this doctrine in declaring "that the government created by this compact was not made the exclusive or final judge of the extent of the powers delegated, since that would have made its discretion and not the constitution the measure of its powers."

Now it may well be said that for the general government to legislate and the states to nullify the legislation a hazardous conflict might be produced, and therefore the power to decide ought to be somewhere. But in fact, as a theoretical question of constitutional law, where is the power? The necessity and the fact are different things. And if the general government may legislate as it thinks proper and also decide upon the validity of the legislation on the ground that the power must be somewhere and that it cannot be intrusted to the states, the states may likewise, theoretically, reply that the power must be somewhere, but cannot be with the general government because they thereby become subject to its discretion. This problem is not yet settled. It will never take the form of nullification again, and it should not. But we may be led to modify our constitution according to the Swiss constitution under which the court cannot invalidate legislation. We may even revert to the principle of the English constitution under which any law is constitutional that parliament enacts. Late republican tendencies which make our constitution a limitation upon power instead of a grant of

power lead inevitably to this end. When congress becomes the judge
of its constitutional energy an enlightened people will hold the balance
of power at the polls.

But the condemnation of Jefferson for his theories of the nature of
the republic is too particular. The charge that he caused the civil war
is a gross absurdity traceable to the fumes of wine. That the states are
sovereign, that the constitution is a compact, that the states may hold
unconstitutional legislation to be void and may adopt such measures as
they think best to protect themselves against it are propositions which
Jefferson held in common with the most eminent men of his time and
they were shared in by many distinguished statesmen since his day.

Hamilton himself, by fair inference, subscribed to the right of secession as early as 1790, eight years before the Kentucky resolutions
were published. Madison, the father of the constitution, was at one with
Jefferson on the resolutions. As early as 1803 the state of Massachusetts
protested against the annexation of Louisiana and declared that "it
formed a new confederacy, to which the states united by the former
compact are not bound to adhere;" and as late as 1844 the same state
resolved that the acquisition of Texas "would have no binding force on
the people of Massachusetts." In 1814 the New England states in the
well-known Hartford convention declared that infractions of the constitution "affecting the sovereignty of a state and liberties of the people"
requires of the "state to interpose its authority for their protection in
the manner best calculated to secure that end" and "states which have
no common umpire must be their own judges and execute their own
designs." This is in part the very language and in entirety the substance
of the Kentucky resolutions. The federalist governors and legislatures
of the New England states shrank in horror from these resolutions in
1798, but in 1814, when the embargo[10] affected the commercial interests
of the New England states, as the alien and sedition laws threatened
the liberties of the whole people without regard to locality, they faced
about and adopted the very blasphemy at which they had held up their
hands so little a time before.

In 1851, after Mr. Webster[11] had sifted these questions with Hayne[12]
and Calhoun, he said: "How absurd it is to suppose that when different
parties enter into a compact for certain purposes either can disregard

any one provision and expect nevertheless the other to observe the rest. *** A bargain cannot be broken on one side and still bind the other side." He was discussing "the union of the states" and the preservation of that union by due observance of the fugitive slave clause[13] of the constitution. In 1848 Mr. Lincoln said in congress: "Any people anywhere, being inclined and having the power, have the right to rise up and shake off the existing government and form a new one that suits them better. Nor is this right confined to cases in which the whole people of an existing government may choose to exercise it. Any portion of such people that can may revolutionize."

Lincoln, of course, was here speaking of the right of revolution. But it does not matter whether secession is accomplished as a compact right or as a revolutionary right so long as it is a right and not a wrong. The compact right is not needed and need not be expressed if the right exists as a revolutionary right. These principles are old and familiar. But it is to be hoped that for all time to come that questions will be settled in the forum and with the ballot. The world has seen enough of force, whether used to suppress or to liberate. The new order of things demands that peace and reason shall prevail. It recognizes human life as sacred. It even looks upon revolution as a doubtful expedient. It therefore reverts to Jefferson's words in the declaration of independence, which caution against revolution for transient causes. Revolution is generally physical force. The triumph of reason ought to and perhaps already has supplanted both.

But enough authority is cited to show that Jefferson did not stand alone in his theories of government, and that he was not a dark and treacherous influence against which all the powers of light were contending. It is a species of childish casuistry[14] to single him out as the author of the nation's woes. This is not the philosophic view of history. Acts and not writings produce revolutions. Men are too taken up with the affairs of their own lives to forsake them under the influence of abstract doctrines. Men react because they are acted upon, and not otherwise.

Happily the question has been settled and no one wants to reopen it. This united republic, if it remains a republic, has a destiny before it immeasurably greater than if the union had been divided. But whether it could be divided and whether laws could be nullified were questions of construction upon which men differed in the early days of the republic and differed frequently upon interest. When states and groups of states north and south at different times subscribed to the principles of the Kentucky resolutions, when Madison, Webster and Lincoln in one form or another advocated them, and when a great majority of the American people elected Jefferson president upon the issue of whether these resolutions were true or false, the denouncement of Jefferson is particular and unjust.

It ill becomes a breed of statesmen who no longer mention the constitution and no longer pretend to observe it to blacken the memory of this great man whose passion for this republic is one of the purest ideals in history and whose defense of the constitution, vigilant and unremitting, rises to the sublimity of heroic legend. Jefferson was a constitutionalist. He believed in the constitution. The party which he founded was and is a constitutional party. Moreover, there has never been any other constitutional party in this country. All other opposing parties, by whatever name they have gone, have done their utmost to undermine the constitution in favor of special privilege, which is the real soul of monarchy.

In Jefferson's day as now public men had to choose between the friendship of monopolists and the friendship of the producers of wealth. Himself of the landed aristocracy of Virginia, his principles were in revolt against special privilege. He doubtless found fewer congenial spirits among those whose cause he championed than he would have found with the federalists.[15] But he made the sacrifice and laid himself liable to the charge of demagogy, which was common even in his day. The federalists hated Jefferson because he stood in their way. He was against their bank and tariff laws and their monarchial tendencies. He exposed their schemes of consolidation and monopoly. His omnipresent influence, subtle and irresistible, baffled them. His pen was never idle; his activities permeated the land. He gathered together the people whose hearts still vibrated with the thunder of liberty and he overthrew the federalists, horse and rider. He clothed abstract principles of justice and equality in such splendor that the popular mind was won from the seductions of power and glory. The federalists found that they were not for America nor America for them. After an interregnum of monarchial drift America resumed its character and destiny. Jefferson as president righted the course of the republic. He became its tutor and trained it so thoroughly that the federalists took to cover. When they emerged it was with a new party, which bore the standard of moral principles triumphant at last by the living influence of him whose memory they abhorred.

Jefferson was at the head of and produced the classical school of American presidents. His principles embellished and strengthened the faculties of men who would have been mediocre without them. He gave form and purpose to the republic. His political canons became law. Madison and Monroe followed in his footsteps. Jackson and Van Buren learned the lesson of government from him. He was the political father of Lincoln. The speeches of every great statesman of this land are saturated with his principles. He set loose a current of liberty which flows around the world today and rocks upon its bosom the toy flotilla[16] of imperialism. The breakers and the depths await it.

Such was the man Jefferson, who thought so little of the office of president that he did not mention it among his achievements. He wanted to be remembered as the author of the declaration of independence, the statute of Virginia for religious freedom and father of the University of Virginia.[17] His long life was spent in the cause of liberty; in disseminating knowledge; in promoting the sciences; in lifting up the weak; in making the world fitter to live in; in constructing for the future. Who disputes his philosophy? Who says that all should not be equal before the law? Who says that men do not have the inalienable rights of life and liberty, that the office of government is to secure these and that governments derive their just powers from the consent of the governed?

His enemies in despair have tortured his kindness into cowardice, his love for humanity into a sordid desire to use the mob. They have called him a shifty doctrinaire. The word means little. But his influence was not bourgeois. He saw the new day; he turned his back on the past. He followed his conscience and the light of his mind to the utmost limits. There was no remnant of monarchy in any of his practices or principles. He is, therefore, in America at least, the one perfect prophet of the future.

Almost to the last day of his life his mind hungered for knowledge and beauty. In the weakness of advanced age, upon the last steps of time, he was reading the bible and the Greek tragedies. His dying hours took him back fifty years through a period of revolution, awakening and progress to the day that was above all others with him. "This is the 4th of July" were the last words he uttered, and he died in the peace of a long and useful life.

Notes

1. A bigot, as defined by the 1906 edition of *Webster's Practical Dictionary*, is "one unreasonably wedded to some religious creed, practice, ritual, etc.; a devotee." Masters uses "bigotry" not to describe prejudice, as modern definitions imply, but to show how Jefferson's work refuted the tyrannical effects of religion over one's intellectual endeavors.

2. On July 8, 1776, Colonel John Nixon first read aloud the Declaration of Independence from the steps of the Pennsylvania State House, now named Independence Hall.

3. In 1890, Republicans in Congress, spearheaded by future president William McKinley, enacted what became known as the McKinley Tariff in an attempt to promote U.S. industrial interests. Later, this protection extended directly to Philippine products entering the U.S. market.

4. The Kentucky Resolutions of 1798, alongside the Virginia Resolutions of the same year, argued that unconstitutional federal laws enacted by Congress may be nullified by the states. See Albert Bushnell Hart and Edward Channing, eds., *The Virginia and Kentucky Resolutions: With the Alien, Sedition, and Other Acts, 1798–1799* (New York: Parker P. Simmons, 1912).

5. Masters is referring here to the creation of a national bank as proposed by Alexander Hamilton in 1791. Jefferson famously opposed Hamilton's argument that the bank constituted "necessary and proper" legislation, as stated in Article I, Section 8, of the Constitution.

6. The Alien and Sedition Acts were a collection of four laws passed by the Federalist-majority Congress in 1798 that targeted people living in the new United States who were not American citizens, called "aliens." Several major changes to U.S. immigration policy were brought about by these acts, including an increase in the number of years of residence required to become a citizen (from five to fourteen) as well as the authorization for the president to deport aliens as he saw fit. The new sedition-related legislation made it illegal to "'print, utter, or publish . . . any false, scandalous, and malicious writing' about the Government."

7. John Taylor of Caroline (1753–1824) was a close friend of Thomas Jefferson, who served as a U.S. senator from 1822 to 1824. Taylor was also responsible for guiding James Madison's Virginia Resolutions through the legislature in 1798.

8. Richard Rush (1780–1859) was a contemporary of Jefferson. He served several presidents in varying capacities, including Madison's comptroller of the Treasury, Monroe's interim secretary of state, Quincy Adams's secretary of the Treasury, and Polk's minister to France.

9. Elbridge Gerry (1744–1814) was James Madison's second vice president and a signer of the Declaration of Independence. The term "gerrymandering" was derived from his name in relation to his time as the governor of Massachusetts.

10. President Jefferson's 1807 Embargo Act closed American ports in an attempt to prevent American involvement in the Napoleonic Wars. See Henry Adams, *The Second Administration of Thomas Jefferson* (New York: Scribner, 1921).

11. Daniel Webster (1782–1852) was a senator and congressman as well as a lawyer who practiced before the U.S. Supreme Court. Webster famously debated Senator Robert Y. Hayne on the topic of states' rights to nullify federal laws.

12. Robert Y. Hayne (1791–1839) was a senator from South Carolina who famously debated Daniel Webster on the topic of states' rights. He supported the rights of individual states to nullify laws they deemed unconstitutional.

13. The Fugitive Slave Clause was included in Article IV of the U.S. Constitution and effectively allowed slaveholders to retrieve the enslaved people who escaped to free states and return them to bondage.

14. "The science of determining the right or wrong of acts and opinions of doubtful propriety." *Webster's Practical Dictionary*, s.v. "casuistry."

15. The Federalists were a political faction formed in 1787 by Alexander Hamilton, John Jay, and James Madison through the creation of the Federalist Papers.

16. "A little fleet, or a fleet of small vessels." *Webster's Practical Dictionary*, s.v. "flotilla."

17. Jefferson was the founder of the University of Virginia in Charlottesville. His religious freedom bill was drafted to promote freedom of conscience for "every denomination."

ALEXANDER HAMILTON

AN American statesman bewitched by the English system; a
revolutionary soldier fighting against the British crown as the
unwilling tories [sic] fought against James II;[1] a monarchist con-
sulting with republicans in the formation of a perfect union of sovereign
states; a thinker whose eyes were clouded with the mist of dissolving
feudalism; a politician unconsciously clinging to the doctrines of divine
right and haunted by a fear of a tumultuary democracy—such a man
gave a lasting impact to the constitution of the only republic of the world.

Alexander Hamilton at 30 years of age was a member of the constitutional convention. He conferred with Washington; he debated
with Madison; he deferred to none. On the contrary, he conjured the
frightful specters of a degraded continental confederacy and played
upon the fears of the stoutest republicans. Among a body of men notable
for intellectual energy, rich in experience and above all trained in the
disquisitions of Locke and Montesquieu, Rousseau and the French
encyclopedists, he launched the schemata of a monarchial system to be
set up in America.[2] Nor was he put down for doing this. He in a sense
succeeded. He imbedded deep in the body of that constitution some
of the germs of monarchy. He nourished them. He founded a school
of political thought which has cherished his memory and blinked at
his principles when it was not safe to avow them openly. And thus his
ghost has stalked throughout the history of the republic.

Hence this is a dramatic episode in political history. The command-ing genius of Jefferson has scarcely been able to divide the control of American polity with the inferior genius of Hamilton. A republic sub-mitting to the incantations of a monarchial thinker is the paradoxical relation which has thriven between Hamilton's influence and the United States.

This complex and fascinating mystery dwarfs the significance of Hamilton's personal career. It is of subordinate consequence that he was indiscreet, vain and opinionated; that he envied Burr's superior success in affairs of the heart; that he published his own amours with a frankness not surpassed by Rousseau; that he boldly advocated a system of governmental corruption; that he was not scrupulous in achieving his ends and that he concocted a scheme to steal the election in the state of New York from Jefferson.[3] To dwell upon these things and to neglect the supreme importance of his political influence would result in missing the main points of his career.

Hamilton's mother was a French woman and to her we trace his refinement, his spirit and his imagination. His father was a Scotchman and from his father he inherited resolution, pertinacity in conviction, great powers of analysis, and a predilection for metaphysics. Thus en-dowed he looked far into the future; he sounded deeply into the tides of destiny; he penetrated the secrets of the human heart and laid hold upon those impulses which from their permanency and strength could be relied upon to carry forward his projects.

Yet his mental construction made him the prey of groundless fears. It led him to assert fallacious premises as the bases of the most elaborate political superstructures. It made him theoretical and impractical. It, in the belief of one great school of thought, veiled with a specious splen-dor a false and indefensible system of government. All his political reasonings were characterized by the fallacy of irrelevant conclusion. He seldom exhausted the contents of a proposition. And therefore his famous dictum that all power should be given neither to the many nor the few has no accurate meaning when analyzed. It fails to include the third term that the only true government is one of law and not of men at all. This is the definition of a republic, a word not understood by him or by many of his contemporaries.

Hamilton had an unreasoning fear of popular institutions. They suggested to him the hybrid experiment of Rome, in which a pure democracy was adulterated with the despotism of mobs and torn by the strife of warring factions. He dwelt upon the fate of the Amphictyonic council;[4] he drew lessons from the history of the German confederacy[5] and the compact of the Swiss cantons.[6] And after traversing the entire field of history he could not escape the conclusion that the United States must be governed by a constitutional monarch. This was his hobby. He bestrode it until his friends were wearied. Even Gouverneur Morris,[7] his most intimate friend and eulogist, wrote: "More a theoretic than a practical man, he was not sufficiently convinced that a system may be good in itself and bad in relation to particular circumstances."[8]

Hamilton could not see that monarchy had its place and its time in the political evolution of man, but that development logically led to popular institutions. In this sense the significance of the English revolution was lost upon him.[9] He could look far into the future and plan for a contingency when his machinations upon human endeavor and sentiment might degenerate a once glorious people into monarchy. But he could not interpret his own age. He was wedded to the past. He worshiped power. He dreaded a free system of government because it might dissolve into anarchy. That a strong government might become despotic did not give him the least concern. Nor could he see that the English system which he affected to admire had not reached the end of its popularization; and that a liberty based upon scripture and a liberty based upon philosophy were co-operating toward a realization of human rights. He abhorred the French revolution as a tragedy of disorder, anarchy and blood. He could not see that it was a great democratic epic which had its place in the history of the world. And so measured by the test of insight, of mental power, of influence upon men and nations, Hamilton was greatly beneath Jefferson. Hamilton believed that the love of gold in man was an energy which could be employed to operate an exclusive system of government. All his measures were fashioned upon the principle of welding the interests of money and government so indissolubly together that the spirit of monarchy would control the body of the republic. And he worked to this end with a patience, a subtlety and a power which have challenged the admiration of all parties.

"He," wrote Senator Lodge, "had been unable to introduce a class influence into the constitution by limiting the suffrage for the president and senate with a property qualification, but by his financial policy he could bring the existing class of wealthy men, comprising at that day the aristocracy bequeathed by provincial times, to the new system and thus, if at all, assure to the property of the country the control of the government."[10] And why was this to be done? As near as we can gather his idea, Hamilton feared that unless the people at large were under the control of a class which possessed the wealth of the country and by that wealth controlled the government, they would plunge forward into anarchy. This system was a mere expedient based upon no principle. For so soon as the people became, if they were not then, intelligent and virtuous the government must settle down through the sands of expediency to the rock of principle. And, taking the people as they were in his day, the question between Jefferson and his school and Hamilton and his school may be reduced to this: Do the prerogatives of equal rights in government furnish a sufficient inspiration to men to preserve law and order by enlisting their selfish motives on the side of their own rights, or must there be a strong party intrenched in power by governmental favor to curb and govern the tumultuary classes? No government can long last in which a majority of the people find their rights ignored, and therefore the preservation of government does depend upon that very interest of the majority in the government which Hamilton could not see was a sufficient cohesion to hold it together. But in any event where is that tumultuary mass which would burst asunder the bonds of restraint if they were weakened?

That millions of farmers who ask nothing from the government in times of peace and give their lives for it in times of war; that millions of artisans the most intelligent of the world; that millions of professional men who pursue their way in life so peaceably as to be unconscious of the barriers of the law—that these, unless restrained by a strong government, will suddenly precipitate disorder and anarchy was the grotesque phantom that haunted the brain of Alexander Hamilton. But it was not more grotesque than most of his reasonings on politics and economics. The question, however, which he had in mind was deeper than he ever expressed it. The strong will overreach the weak; the fit will survive. Shall government, then, be instituted to secure justice? No; government shall be instituted to protect the strong in what they have obtained; to curb an uprising of those who have been wronged in the race of life; to cow that discontent and subdue that disorder which never arose out of mere malice and wantonness, but always as a reaction against oppression, and, in short, to redouble the vigor of the law of the survival of the fittest in order to crush into tributary submission the men whose industry produces national wealth. Hence Hamilton admired the British system, because he conceived it to contain those checks which, within the pale of law and order, restrained the rapacity of the patricians and the rebellion of the plebeians.[11] He saw in the house of lords a body of men having nothing to hope for by any change, endowed with vast property by the government and therefore faithful to the government which had purchased their friendship and, so constituted, forming a barrier against the aggression of the crown and the clamor of the commons.[12] But we know that Hamilton's estimate of the house of lords was unsupported by history. He was about 30 years of age when he made this argument in the constitutional convention. It is impossible to conceive that it did not amuse such scholars as Madison and Franklin.

Hamilton favored the model of the English executive. He contended that the interest of a king is so interwoven with that of the nation and his personal emolument so great that he was placed above the danger of being corrupted from abroad.[13] On the other hand, one of the weak sides of republics was their being liable to foreign influence and corruption. He did not call to mind the alliance between Mary of England and Philip II of Spain,[14] nor that of James II and Louis XIV,[15] nor that Charles II was a pensioner of the great French despot.[16] Nor did he consider that in an elective government no alliance between a president and a foreign ruler could be certain or long reliable. That such a contingency has never been even approximated in this country except when Hamilton's peculiar influence was ascendant is sufficient proof that Hamilton's argument was purely theoretic and fantastic. But while he pictured the independence of the house of lords he insisted as a political principle that if we expect men to serve the public their passions must be interested. Hence he applauded that patronage which proceeded from the crown, denominated by David Hume[17] as corruption, as the influence which maintained the equilibrium of the British constitution.

Aside from the unsoundness of these principles their ethical baseness cannot be sufficiently condemned. They involve the fallacy of doing evil that good may come. They constitute a scheme of homeopathy[18] in governmental polity. Petty larceny is to be cured by grand larceny. Private dishonor is to be prevented by public plunder. Men who are capable of thriving above their fellows under any condition are to receive special aid and immunity from the state in order to win their adherence to it. The design presupposes that the strong will not impart their support to a government unless the government first gives them the chief seats and doles out its patronage to them. No account is taken of the better element of human nature, but only of the passions of greed and power. The vast millions who are to be governed and who will raise the revenue for this perfect state must be held in abeyance by a strong military which Hamilton championed with great energy in the convention in order that their anarchistic impulses may have no chance to find expression.

Such a plan could not fail to be immensely successful. As far as history furnishes any record the human race has persistently struggled against the temptation of money. Evangels and prophets have exhorted against the love of money as the root of all evil. That love remains an ineradicable passion in man. Hence a political creed that promised to the faithful bounties and subsidies, privileges and immunities has gained the support of millions. The mixture of fallacy and tergiversation,[19] corruption and greed was brewed into a broth which has brought toil to the masses and trouble to those who seek to press the cup to the lips of a reluctant civilization.

At each anniversary of Hamilton's birth the postprandial orators praise him as a constructive statesman. Was he in truth constructive? Does his scheme tend to strengthen individual character and morality? Does it give hope to the better aspirations of humanity? Does it elevate the race? Does it assist man in his difficult ascent to the heights of a better day? Is it in accord with Christianity? Is there justice in it, or mercy or faith? Or is it armed with fraud and wrong, and masked with the mummery of a hideous skepticism; a skepticism that parades this world as the only theater of hope? These questions must be answered by everyone who cares to read the utterances of Hamilton in the constitutional convention, in his letters, in his state papers and in the faithful reports of his friends.

Hamilton's hobby was to effect consolidation in the government and make it strong. The means by which he proposed to do this was to array property on the side of government. To array property on the side of government he designed to burden the people. His scheme was constructive so far as it built up a plutocracy and strengthened the government. But it was destructive of the people themselves. Hence in accepting or rejecting Hamilton a choice must be made between an artificial body known as the state, created by man as a means to an end, and man himself, who formed the state not for his own oppression, but for the establishment of equity.

Those who look askance upon republican institutions will not deplore the degenerating influence of Hamilton's attacks upon the constitution. They imagine that his genius evolved a true government out of that constitution which was the product of the greatest assembly of men in the history of the United States. And, of course, they are thankful for that. But, moreover, it is urged that the means themselves which Hamilton employed to bring about that consolidation evinced a commanding genius for finance and political economy and as commercial polities were themselves as vital breath. But his national bank had its prototype in the Bank of St. George at Genoa, the Bank of Amsterdam and the Bank of England. Its interests—like the Bank of England—were designed to be coincident with those of the government. Thereby the money of the country was to be brought to the side of the government. Even to details the bank was not an original conception. The charter contained many of the conditions which parliament had imposed upon the incorporators of the English bank. It was given a monopoly of the national banking business. It could issue paper money. For the virtue of this, Hamilton argued, was to keep the precious metals in the vaults, because when they circulated they became so much dead stock. Such were his ideas upon the subject of money. But they were in harmony with the zealous convictions which he held upon the solecism of a favorable balance of trade, which he worshiped with an ardor approaching the Egyptian reverence for onions and cats. When Hamilton was called upon to defend his banking scheme to President Washington he submitted a written argument in answer to the objections of Jefferson, which, for ingenuity, subtlety and power, did credit to his peculiar mind. Indeed, it overmatched the somewhat desultory and inconclusive paper of Jefferson. The question was: Does the constitution permit congress to incorporate such a bank?

Today the question would be: Is banking a governmental function? Is a national bank an economic utility? Washington was seriously perplexed by the reasons urged for and against the bank, and while he was deliberating upon it the question arose how the ten days clause of the constitution for the president's approval of a bill was to be construed.[20] Hamilton argued that the day of its presentation was to be excluded and the last day also. It resulted that Washington held the bill for eleven days and on the eleventh day approved it. And so a part of Hamilton's collateral plan to overthrow the constitution was accomplished.

Of Hamilton's funding scheme it is only necessary to say that he meant to create a permanent public debt. This was that reservoir into which the money of plutocracy was to be poured, so favorably built and placed as to draw to itself the wealth of the unsuspecting people. Historians relate in triumphant tones that England's prosperity has kept pace with her increasing debt. And the economists have been made the butt of ridicule by men who call themselves practical. The former assert that an increasing public debt will eventually overwhelm any nation. The latter reply that an increasing public debt is a means to prosperity and that it adds strength to the government. In olden times there was supposed to be a causal relation between the conjunction of planets and a national calamity. Sometimes national prosperity is attributed to national character; not taking into account abundant minerals and coal, a fertile soil and a favorable climate, national harbors and means of commerce.

Children associate fortune with a four-leafed clover. And all mercantilists of which Hamilton was a confirmed disciple believe that a national debt is a source of prosperity; that taxing ourselves makes us rich. So the protective tariff,[21] also inaugurated by Hamilton, has clung to the United States in spite of all efforts to throw it off. Whenever the people have voted it out they repent the act and invite it back. When more men are wiser and when those who are wiser are more candid the attempt to confuse public thought on the questions of balance of trade, public debt, government banks, paper money, tariffs, subsidies, bounties and special privilege as efficient means of prosperity will decrease. There will then be an advance beyond the pale of the seventeenth century in economics. If the foregoing plans are constructive, then Hamilton is entitled to the immortal reverence of the American people.

But is not a spirit of justice pervading all systems and all polities the only constructive force? Can a great nation be constructed except by building up its people as a whole? At least more than half of the people of both England and the United States believe that justice and equality applied to these subjects are the only curatives. They are not sufficiently organized or cohesive, however, to push forward with much speed against casual undertows and countervailing currents.

While Hamilton and Jefferson were not political friends no man has spoken more favorably of the former than the founder of the democratic party. In the much abused "Anas"[22] Jefferson wrote in 1818: "Hamilton was indeed a singular character. Of acute understanding, disinterested, honest and honorable in all private transactions, amiable in society and duly valuing virtue in private life, yet so bewitched and perverted by the British example as to be under thorough conviction that corruption was essential to the government of a nation." And to Benjamin Rush[23] he wrote: "Hamilton believed in the necessity of either force or corruption to govern men."

Hamilton and Burr had maligned each other for years. This hatred culminated in a duel. Hamilton fell. Gouverneur Morris pronounced his funeral oration, gliding with trepidation over the dark places in the great man's career. His body was buried in Trinity churchyard at the foot of Wall street, where imagination may picture his spirit hovering over the temple of English monarchy and peering down one of the greatest money centers of the world.

Notes

1. James II, king of England, Ireland, and Scotland (1633–1701), was over-thrown because of his Catholic tendencies by Dutch leader, William of Orange (1650–1702) during the Glorious Revolution (1688–89) with the support of Par-liament. Tories supported the king's hereditary right to the throne, though ultimately many Tories came to support the revolution that overthrew James II. See Gary S. DeKrey, *Restoration and Revolution in Britain: A Political History of the Era of Charles II and the Glorious Revolution* (New York: Palgrave Macmillan, 2007).

2. All of these names mentioned are philosophers of the Enlightenment who influenced the making of the American Constitution. John Locke (1632–1704) was an English philosopher who claimed that the three natural rights of an individual were life, liberty, and estate. Baron de Montesquieu (1689–1755) was a French philosopher who promoted the idea of the separation of powers. Jean-Jacques Rousseau (1712–78) was a Geneva-born philosopher who intro-duced the social contract theory. The French Encyclopedists, two of whom were Montesquieu and Rousseau, worked together to create the *Encyclopédie* whose goal to gather general knowledge within a single publication, represented the ideals of the Enlightenment.

3. Alexander Hamilton (1757–1804), during the presidential election of 1800, encouraged John Jay, then governor of New York, to change the way in which New York electors were chosen. *The Papers of Alexander Hamilton: From Alexander Hamilton to John Jay*, Harold C. Syrett, ed. (New York: Columbia University Press, 1976), 464–67.

4. In ancient Greece, the Amphictyonic Council was a coalition of states, already ancient during the heyday of the polis system, which were who were dissolved by Philip II of Macedonia (382 BCE–336 BCE).

5. The German Confederacy was a political coalition established by the Con-gress of Vienna to replace the Holy Roman Empire.

6. The Swiss cantons are independent states in Switzerland that form a league without any imperial authority. This league is still present as of 2021.

7. Gouverneur Morris (1752–1816) was a contemporary of Hamilton and one of the Founding Fathers of the United States. He was nicknamed the "Penman of the Constitution" for his hand in creating the language of the Constitution.

8. From an 1804 letter to Governor Aaron Ogden.

9. King Charles I (1600–1649), who believed in divine right of rulers, dismissed Parliament. This spurred the English Civil War, which lasted from 1642 to 1651.

10. Masters here quotes Henry Cabot Lodge (1850–1924), senator of Massachu-setts, from his biography, *Alexander Hamilton* (Boston: Houghton, 1882), 90–91.

11. The British system Masters is referring to is that of the British Constitution, which consisted of the hereditary monarch, a House of Lords, and a House of Commons.

12. The House of Lords was the branch of British Parliament that represented the hereditary aristocracy.

13. Emolument is defined as the profit one receives from their employment. *Webster's Practical Dictionary*, (Springfield, MA: G & C Merriam Co., 1906), s.v. "emolument." 126.

14. Mary (1516–1558) and Phillip II (1527–1598) of Spain were matched in together as apart of an arranged marriage to help further the prospects of both kingdoms.

15. James II, King of England, Ireland, and Scotland (1633-1701) was cousin and ally to Louis XIV, king of France (1638–1715). James II tried to model his government after that of Louis XIV's; however, after failing to reinstate Catholicism into the country, Louis XIV aided him financially and politically.

16. Masters here is referring to the Secret Treaty of Dover that Charles II, king of Scotland, England, and Ireland (1630–85), had with France. In the treaty, Charles II supported French policy in exchange for a yearly pension as well as protection by French troops if ever needed.

17. David Hume (1711–76) was a Scottish philosopher during the Enlightenment.

18. Homeopathy is a medical term describing the practice of giving small doses of a medicine to cure an afflicted patient; large doses of this same medicine would cause a healthy person to experience the symptoms of the disease. *Webster's Practical Dictionary*, s.v. "homeopathy."

19. Tergiversation is a "fickleness of conduct." *Webster's Practical Dictionary*, s.v. "tergiversation." 443.

20. The ten days clause, otherwise known as the Presentment Clause, found in Article I, Section 7, of the Constitution, states that after being presented a bill passed by both Houses, the president only has only ten days to return a decision on the bill back to Congress.

21. Alexander Hamilton (1757–1804) first proposed the use of protective tariffs in his *Report on the Subject of Manufactures*, written in 1791. Hamilton believed that tariffs on imported items would encourage Americans to begin manufacturing such items at home.

22. Masters here is referencing the collection of personal notes, documents, and letters put together by former United States president, Thomas Jefferson (1743–1826). The word "ana" is defined as being a suffix that can be added to a name to signify, "a collection of memorable sayings"; it can also stand alone as a noun, as used here. *Webster's Practical Dictionary*, s.v. "ana." 14.

23. Benjamin Rush (1746–1813) was one of the signatories of the Declaration of Independence.

IMPLIED POWERS
AND IMPERIALISM

NO "progressive development" of the constitution can ever obliterate its original character and meaning upon many of its important features. This is true because its authors employed language as a whole which is remarkably clear; and the proceedings of state conventions and the writings of contemporary statesmen furnish additional data for construction and exposition. Thus the federal principle of the United States government is one of the most conspicuous things in the constitution. The constitution was adopted by states, it was to be binding between states when nine had ratified it, and it was to be amended by states. The senators, first called ambassadors, were to represent states. The president was to be elected by electors from states. The federal courts were to decide controversies between citizens of different states, and controversies where conflicting claims of different states were involved. Though development may wipe out the practical effects of these principles of the constitution, history cannot be obscured. So long as writings exist the original nature of the government will be clear to any man who can read.

Nor can any ingenuity argue away the fact that the United States government was created as a government of special and limited powers. For the ninth amendment to the constitution reads: "The enumeration in the constitution of certain rights shall not be construed to deny or disparage others retained by the people." This is a most pregnant provision. For it is equivalent to saying that the failure to deny a power in the general government shall not be construed to grant it. It means that the constitution is not a limitation upon power. Directly bearing upon the limited character of this government is the Tenth amendment which reads "the powers not delegated to the United States nor prohibited by it to the states are reserved to the states respectively or to the people." Human speech is not capable of more precise meanings than these clauses convey. How did they come to be inserted in the constitution?

A confederation of states comprising a population of some 3,000,000 people had repelled an army of subjugation, and had returned to the walks of civil life. This birth of freedom brought its reaction. The aristocracy never wanted war with England. After it was over the cynical and selfish elements of the people hastened the dying down of the patriotic fires.[1] The war had interrupted business and now to return to practical questions since the country was cut loose from the parent government, treaties must be made, commerce must resume its offices, and the United States must take their place as an entity in the world. If that day could be reconstructed in imagination the people as a whole would be seen going their way in the usual routine of life as happy and contented as they have done since under the constitution. People and not charters are the realities of life. Little credit can be given by the philosophic historian to the claim that the people were drifting toward anarchy because the articles of confederation contained defects—defects which did not break down the people during a period of war and revolution. But conceding that changes in the organic law[2] were needful and important the convention-call expressed the purpose of "revising the articles of confederation." The commercial interests demanded the revision. In order that the States could act with unity in foreign relations it was necessary that the general government should have more direct powers; for in such things energy and celerity[3] are prerequisites of safety.

The constitution created a form of government never known before. There had been successful confederacies before the American confederacy, and the latter was certainly successful. These confederacies fell through the decay of the particular sentiment which gave them birth. The American confederacy was unified, it was given the spirit by the impulse of liberty which had been enkindled by oppression. Once the revolution was over the spirit of liberty subsided to some extent from a national channel, through the removal of the cause that drew it there and returned to more local and more individual and therefore more practical channels. It is probably beyond the capacity of the human intellect to determine whether if no change had been made in the form of the government the legitimate development of the people would have been different from what it turned out to be. If the people could once unite in a confederacy and save themselves they could do so again so long as they kept the spirit of independence; and when that is gone neither institutions nor constitutions will forestall foreign rule.

The form of government created by the constitution is novel in this that it is both confederative and national. Out of confederated states rises a distinct entity concerned with functions which it has been empowered by the states to perform; and this entity is divided according to the principles of Montesquieu[4] into the departments of legislative, executive and judicial, acting within their delegated powers as if a general government had been created which had obliterated every feature of the confederacy. In this creation a step was taken beyond any former attempt. It was an evolutionary development beyond the philosophy of all political thinkers who lived before that day.

The necessity for revising the old articles of confederation was felt on all hands; but at the same time the people feared that the benefits of the revolution might be lost through the creation of a centralized government. The sedate, the orderly, the conservative elements of society, the people who amass wealth and attain position and power through its influence, complained of the excesses of democracy. They took advantage of the disorder which follows a war, the embarrassment which accompanies interrupted commerce to argue in favor of a stronger government. And all the ills which afflicted the new republic attributable not to the form of government entirely but to events from which they logically flowed were charged to the weakness of the confederacy. Nevertheless the hostility against the creation of a central government in which local self government would be engulfed was so great that out of sixty-five delegates selected to attend the constitutional convention sixteen failed to appear. Patrick Henry declined the appointment altogether; and ten refused to sign the constitution after it was formulated. Of the three delegates sent by New York two returned when they feared that the convention was proceeding not to revise the articles of confederation but to go much beyond that in the formation of a government unknown and probably of doubtful power. These facts demonstrate the feelings of the most thoughtful people of the time and their aversion to a government which could be tortured by construction or development into an engine of oppression.[5]

But Mr. Madison in Article 44 of the Federalist[6] insisted that the constitution invigorated the powers of the articles of confederacy, and added but a few new powers. These he said were the power to raise revenue by taxes directly levied upon the people; the power to make naturalization laws uniform throughout the United States, and like uniform laws of bankruptcy; the power to issue patents and copyrights and the power to regulate trade with foreign nations, and among the several states. New restraints upon the states prohibited them from emitting bills of credit, or making anything but gold or silver legal tender in the payment of debts; prohibiting them from passing any bill of attainder or *ex post facto*[7] law, or law impairing the obligation of contracts; or from laying any imposts or duties upon imports or granting any title of nobility. Under the constitution the states control their militia and Congress can only organize them, arm them and call them out for service. Under the articles of confederation Congress had the power to appoint all the officers of the state militia; while under the constitution Congress cannot appoint these officers, but their appointments rest with the states whether the militia be in service or not. Outside of these provisions the constitution is a replica of the Articles of Confederation in respect to the powers created in either. The federal judiciary was a new feature, but the constitution invested it with powers which Congress exercised under the articles of confederation.

But by the articles of confederation it was provided that "every power, jurisdiction and right which is not by this confederation expressly delegated to the United States in Congress assembled"[8] is retained by each state. The constitution did not contain such a provision. On the contrary after granting all the old powers except as noted Congress was empowered to make all laws "which shall be necessary and proper for carrying into execution the foregoing powers."[9] This became known as the "sweeping clause" in the discussions upon the constitution when it went to the states for ratification.

The history of the "sweeping clause" is as follows: On the second working day of the convention, May 29, 1787, Charles Pinckney, delegate from South Carolina offered a draft of a constitution which almost in substance and largely in language was the instrument finally approved by the convention. William Patterson of New Jersey also offered a draft which was considered and debated upon. A committee appointed from the body was instructed to consider the Pinckney and Patterson plans, which consisted of John Rutledge of South Carolina, Edmund Randolph of Virginia, Nathaniel Gorham of Massachusetts, Oliver Ellsworth of Connecticut and James Wilson of Pennsylvania. Of the five three were accomplished lawyers.

Pinckney's plan, after providing for power in Congress to declare war, provide for the common defense, and to do other things much as the grant stood in the constitution as adopted, invested Congress with power as follows:

"And make all laws for carrying the foregoing powers into execution."[10]

The committee in question reported on August 6, 1787, after giving both plans thorough consideration and submitting each clause to rigid scrutiny. In the draft that they reported back to the convention they amended the clause just quoted so as to read:

"To make all laws that shall be necessary and proper for carrying into execution the foregoing powers," etc.

The committee had inserted the words "necessary and proper" and had improved the rhetoric of the Pinckney clause. In this form it went before the people for adoption.

In the Virginia state convention which ratified the constitution Edmund Randolph, who was a member of the committee which inserted the words "necessary and proper" hastened to assure the people that the clause was harmless. It was, he said, a safeguard against monopolies. "This fundamental clause," said he, "does not in the least increase the powers of Congress. It is only inserted for greater caution. No sophistry will be permitted to explain away these powers, nor can they possibly assume any other power, but what is contained in the constitution without usurpation."

In the same convention Patrick Henry declared that "when men give power they know not what they give." And of those who argued that the exercise of power which he feared would never be resorted to, he asked "why give power so totally unnecessary that it is said it will never be used?"

Edmund Pendleton on June 14, 1788, also made a speech on the "sweeping clause." "I understand that clause as not going a single step beyond the delegated powers. What can it act upon? Some power given by the constitution. If they should be about to pass a law in consequence of this clause they must pursue some of the delegated powers, but can by no means depart from them, or arrogate any new powers for the plain language of the clause is to give them power to pass laws in order to give effect to the delegated powers."

George Mason wanted an amendment so as to make the point clear; but amendments to this clause which to many minds was already perspicuous beyond doubt seemed caution run mad; and as the whole convention was agreed upon an amendment declaring that powers not delegated were reserved the question seemed to be covered completely. Notwithstanding this George Nicholas wished an amendment to be introduced in order to remove all apprehensions. John Marshall who was present, and who by an almost dramatic irony of fate was to construe the clause in question as Chief Justice of the Supreme Court, lent his influence to quiet the panic: "The State governments," he said, "did not derive their powers from the general government, but each government derived its powers from the people, and each was to act according to the powers given it." Then adverting to "the sweeping clause" he said, "Does not a power remain until it is given away?"

Such were the deliberations of Marshall's own state, deliberations in which he joined, and deliberations to which he contributed the weight of his influence in persuading a cautious and reserved people, fresh from revolution, to have no fear of the new government.

James Wilson had insisted in the Pennsylvania Convention on November 24, 1787, that all power resided in the people, and that the words: "We, the people," meant a grant from the whole people for the purposes of a common government. And it followed as a necessary corollary from his premises that whatever power was not granted by the people was retained by the people, except as they may have surrendered it to the several states.

While the constitution was pending before the states Jay, Madison and Hamilton were publishing a series of articles in the New York papers in favor of the new constitution.[11] On January 3, 1788, one of these, written by Hamilton, appeared in the Daily Advertiser, and in discussing the "sweeping clause" Hamilton said:

"It conducts us to this palpable truth that a power to lay and collect taxes must be a power to pass laws necessary and proper for the execution of that power; and what does the unfortunate and calumniated provision do more than declare the same truth, to wit; that the national legislature to whom the power of laying and collecting taxes had been previously given, might in the execution of that power pass all laws necessary and proper to carry it into effect." * * *[12] "The declaration itself, though it may be chargeable with tautology or redundancy is at least perfectly harmless."[13]

If Hamilton were right in this and the people felt assured upon the subject they had no reason to fear that twenty years after Marshall would hold that the "necessary and proper" clause "purports to enlarge and not to diminish the powers vested in the government" and "purports to be an additional power and not a restriction."[14]

In any deliberative assembly there is a compound of diverse prejudices and convictions. All minds do not perceive the fundamental, the essential. Some see the subsidiary, the accidental and couple with their imperfect perception energy to demand and eagerness to debate. Any organic law is the product of such warring minds. And besides a constitution cannot from its character contain much detail. If it descends to trifles, to ways and means; if it is overloaded with restrictions and exceptions and qualified by still others for greater certainty it becomes a prolix[15] puzzle which only the very learned and the very patient can comprehend. But there is such a thing as mental integrity, which forbids construing an instrument of freedom into a charter of despotism. No constitution can be drawn by the wit of man which cannot be forged into a weapon of wrong and oppression by loquacious sophistry. Subtleties may confound the plainest truths and arguments be advanced to justify any pretension, however repugnant to justice. So that in the last analysis morality becomes the final arbiter of a people's fate. The most careful system will collapse under the assaults of intriguing and unscrupulous special privilege. It is left to us to infer that such general considerations as forbade the formation of a mere code, overcame the recommendations of the states on the subject of an amendment prohibiting commercial monopolies. If all powers not granted were reserved, the most prophetic insight could not have foreseen that the power to erect a "commercial monopoly" could be drawn from powers "necessary and proper" to the execution of enumerated powers. The amendments which were adopted at the instigation of the suspicious and reluctant states were of a character calculated to satisfy the most critical.

Again it was generally known that the power to create corporations had been expressly raised in the constitutional convention and rejected. And if in the language of Marshall in the Virginia convention a "power remains until it is given away" no power was given away which was expressly proposed and expressly denied. Marshall's dictum was true even if there had been silence on the subject; how much truer was it when the convention had spoken its negative to the grant of power to create corporations. This action of the convention was generally known; for many of its members returned to their respective states to become members of the state conventions for adoption, and brought with them intimate knowledge and quickened intelligence upon the constitution and its meaning.

In fact Mr. Madison on August 18, 1787, submitted to the convention to be referred to the committee on detail certain powers to be added to those of the general legislature among which was the following:

"To grant charters of incorporation in cases where the public good may require them and the authority of a single state may be incompetent."

On September 14, 1787, Dr. Franklin moved to add after the words: "Post roads" (Art. I, Sec. 8) a grant of power "to provide for cutting canals where deemed necessary."

Mr. Madison then added to Dr. Franklin's motion a power which he had submitted on August 18th, as already stated "to grant charters of incorporation where the interests of the United States might require and the legislative provisions of individual states may be incompetent."

"Mr. Randolph seconded the proposition."

"Mr. King thought the power unnecessary. The states will be prejudiced and divided into parties about it. In Philadelphia and New York it will be referred to the establishment of a bank, which has been a subject of contention in those cities. In other places it will be referred to mercantile monopolies."

* * * * * * * * *

"The question being so modified as to admit a distinct question specifying and limited to the case of canals the vote was taken with the following result: Pennsylvania, Virginia and Georgia—Aye, 3; New Hampshire, Massachusetts, Connecticut, New Jersey, Delaware, Maryland, North Carolina and South Carolina, No, 8. The whole matter fell." As seen two southern states and one northern state voted aye; five northern states and three southern states voted no.

The states were not satisfied with the argument that powers not given away are retained although historically and legally it was perfectly valid. The dread of mercantile monopolies and of banks, the fear that silence in the constitution might be used against the states for the creation of corporations in general by Congress led them to suggest amendments to the constitution which would prevent the exercise of such power. It was an act of caution characteristic of human nature, but logically was out of place. For as under the articles of confederation each state retained its sovereignty and every power not expressly granted, and as they had not in the constitution parted with their sovereignty but had only granted certain sovereign powers or incidents of sovereignty it could not be necessary to negative the grant of something which could not pass. The precautionary language in fact lent color to a specious claim that the new government was something different than it really was.

Massachusetts was one of the first states to ratify the constitution; and its action preceded that of South Carolina or Virginia by several months. And in its instrument of ratification it was declared that:

"It is the opinion of this convention that certain amendments and alterations in the said constitution would remove the fears and quiet the apprehensions of many of the good people of this commonwealth, and more effectually guard against an undue administration of the federal government."

And the convention recommended as amendments:

I. "That it be explicitly declared that all powers not expressly delegated by the aforesaid constitution are reserved to the several states to be by them exercised.

V. "That Congress erect no company of merchants with exclusive advantages of commerce."

New Hampshire ratified the constitution before Virginia and in its instrument of ratification it was set forth:

"As it is the opinion of the convention that certain amendments and alterations in the said constitution would remove the fears and quiet the apprehensions of many of the good people of this state and more effectually guard against an undue administration of the federal government."

It was recommended that the following amendments to the constitution be made:—

I. "That it be explicitly declared that all powers not expressly and particularly delegated by the aforesaid constitution are reserved to the several states to be by them exercised."

V. "That Congress shall erect no company of merchants with exclusive advantages of commerce."

John Marshall was a member of the Virginia state convention and participated in its debates. Virginia ratified the constitution on June 26, 1788, a month after South Carolina ratified it, and a month before New York ratified it and in its instrument of ratification the people of Virginia said:

"With these impressions" that "every power not granted thereby remains with them and at their will" and that nothing can be done by the house and senate or the president "except in those instances in which power is given for those purposes" they accepted the constitution.

South Carolina ratified the constitution on May 23, 1788, and its convention declared that:

"This convention doth also declare that no section or paragraph of said constitution warrants a construction that the states do not retain every power not expressly relinquished by them," etc.

New York ratified the constitution on July 26, 1788, and its convention incorporated in the instrument of ratification these words:

"That every power, jurisdiction and right which is not by the said constitution clearly delegated to the congress of the United States or the departments of the government thereof remains to the people of the several states." * * * * "Clauses which deny powers do not imply powers not so negatived, but are exceptions to specified powers or are inserted for greater caution."

And it was recommended as an amendment:

"That the Congress do not grant monopolies or erect any company with exclusive advantages of commerce."

Of the nine states which first adopted the constitution, nine being necessary to establish it, New Hampshire was last. Three of the original nine made recommendations as already noticed for specific amendments in order to preserve local powers and to limit the constitutional grant. Two of these were northern states and one was a southern state. Massachusetts, the home of Puritanism, led off as shown with declarations and amendments and New Hampshire followed her example using almost the same language of the Massachusetts ratification. New York, which was the eleventh state in point of time to ratify the constitution, proposed amendments as already appears and of the eleven states which had ratified the constitution by March 4, 1789, five had proposed amendments of limitation and of these three were northern states and two were southern states. Rhode Island, which adopted the constitution on May 29, 1790, declared in its instrument of ratification that:

"Every power, jurisdiction and right which is not by the said constitution clearly delegated to the congress of the United States," etc., "remains to the people," and the convention recommended an amendment providing:

"That Congress erect no company with exclusive privileges of commerce."

The revolutionary spirit, the consciousness of liberty dearly bought prompted these suggested amendments. They were inspired by jealousy, by an intuition of human nature with its passions for power. The courageous men who disregarded the ties of friendship, the amenities of conventional debate, and who impugned the judgment or good faith of their associates to secure these amendments can never be honored sufficiently by a grateful people. "Is a power not retained until it is given away?" asked Marshall. "Why not say so?" retorted Patrick Henry; "Is it because it will consume too much paper? * * * Nations who have trusted to logical deductions have lost their liberty. * * * I see the awful immensity of the dangers with which it (the constitution) is pregnant. I see it; I feel it!" A fearful storm broke as Mr. Henry was concluding, driving the convention into a panic. It was his last speech. Nevertheless the work had been done. The timorous, the trusting, the indifferent, the sophists, the monocrats[16] were overridden. On March 4, 1789, the first day of the new government, Congress passed a resolution which among other things contained this language:

"The conventions of a number of the states having at the time of their adopting the constitution expressed a desire in order to prevent misconstruction and abuse of its powers, that further declaratory and restrictive clauses should be added; and as extending the ground of public confidence in the government will best insure the beneficent ends of its institutions," it was resolved that among others these two amendments be proposed to the legislatures of the states:

"The enumeration in the constitution of certain rights shall not be construed to deny or disparage others retained by the people."

"The powers not delegated, to the United States by the constitution, nor prohibited by it, to the states are reserved to the states respectively or to the people."[17]

Thus the character of the government was not left to be ascertained by logical deduction. Its character was stamped in plain language upon the constitution of the government, and nothing could have changed it except wilful violation of the instrument.

The subjects upon which the doctrine of implied powers was first invoked, namely, the protective tariff, and a United States bank, have been obscured by the graver questions of colonialism and militarism.[18]

But as the reasoning which was used to support the tariff and the bank is the same which was used to support colonialism and will be use to further revolutionize the form of the government, an examination of its futile sophistry cannot be out of place.

If the constitution as proposed had contained a clause empowering congress to grant charters of incorporation no question could ever have been raised to the bank except one of expediency. Madison, as shown, seemed to think it a proper power for congress to possess. Objections might have been made afterwards to the propriety of a banking corporation chartered by congress. Some might have thought state banks sufficient. But if the constitution enumerated the power its exercise would have been like that of the power to pass general bankruptcy laws, sometimes to be availed of and at other times to be relinquished to the states.

It is past all doubt, however, that the framers of the constitution were exceedingly apprehensive of corporations; and the danger suggested to their minds in the concrete was commercial monopolies, such as the East India Company of England, which was to them what the trusts are to us to-day. Monopolies of one kind or another, but all relating to commerce, had always afflicted England, as well as other countries. And this they no doubt sought to forestall as to America. Besides they could see as clearly as we can now that national corporations would look to their creator for protection and redress; they would proceed from the general government, but would roam at will through the states. They might be even banking corporations and as shown anything in the constitution squinting towards a bank suggested defeat in its adoption by New York and Pennsylvania. They would have little, perhaps nothing, to ask from the states; at least the question was so doubtful that those who framed the constitution declined to incur any risk on the subject. Besides the abstract right of local control was a touchstone in determining every grant of power which the constitution contained. So much power as was necessary to accomplish national purposes was intended to be given away; and all in excess of that was to be retained. It was perfectly obvious also that a corporation involved some form of special privilege, either by way of exceptions to the person interested, or by way of centralized power for corporate purposes. What sort of bodies would emanate from the general government under such a constitutional power? They could foresee great trading companies and great banks. The right to charter carries with it the right to grant privileges and franchises. And what state could protect itself against such an incorporeal creature when no state could control the power which gave it existence? Hence, as already shown, congress was denied the power to charter companies.

As congress possesses definite powers expressed with rhetorical precision, the creation of a corporation not only must raise the question of the expediency and justice of the particular act; it must also lead men to inquire what limit can be set to congressional action. If the constitution can be broken down for a good purpose it can be broken down for a bad purpose. And whether the purpose be good or bad, the methods essential to employ in levelling the constitutional barriers are among the most corrupt as they are the most dangerous that ingenious lawlessness can devise. To say, for instance, that congress can constitutionally impose a protective tariff under the general power "to promote the general welfare" or that it may incorporate a bank under the general clause empowering congress "to lay and collect taxes," because a bank may by possibility through its functions of deposit and transmission facilitate the collection of taxes, is a form of illogic, the danger of which cannot be estimated. Joseph Story, in writing upon the protective tariff, had occasion to advert to the pernicious subtleties with which these arguments are clothed. "The violation," wrote he, "consists in using a power granted for one object to advance another, and that by a sacrifice of the original object. It is, in a word, a violent perversion, the most dangerous of all, because the most insidious and difficult to resist."

In August of 1790 congress called upon Hamilton as Secretary of the Treasury to report further provision for establishing the public credit. On December 13, 1790, Hamilton responded by furnishing to congress his first report on a national bank. This report need not engage our attention because it related to the expediency of such an institution and the details of its formation. In conformity with the report the legislative bill of creation was formulated in congress and provoked instant and bitter hostility.

We have already seen that Madison was not opposed to corporations of themselves, but on the contrary thought congress might have the power to charter them. But when the convention overruled him and the constitution went into force devoid of any such powers Madison evinced the courage and good faith to stand by the constitution as it was adopted. The congressional debates disclose that on February 2, 1791, Madison made a speech on the bank bill in opposition to it. "He then expressly denied the power of congress to establish banks. And this he said was not a novel opinion; he had long entertained it. All power, he said, had its limits; those of the general government were ceded from the mass of general power inherent in the people, and were consequently confined within the limits fixed by their act of cession."[19]

Hamilton's elaborate argument contained in his report to congress in which he set out the constitutional provisions and deductions supposed to authorize the chartering of the bank is an adroit piece of fallacious reasoning. Thus his first proposition involves the fallacy of undistributed middle. It is this: that the United States are sovereign and as all sovereign nations can incorporate companies the United States as a sovereign nation can incorporate a bank. The major term here is: the United States are a sovereign nation; and the minor term is: a sovereign nation may incorporate a bank; and the conclusion is: the United States may incorporate a bank. But the minor premise which declares that a sovereign nation may incorporate a bank means a nation which is sovereign as to all subjects, while the major premise can only mean that the United States are sovereign with respect to some subjects, that is, it can exercise only a limited amount of sovereignty. Thus the fallacy consists in using the words "sovereign nation" and "United States" as equivalent terms. There is a play upon words using the terms first in one sense and then secondly in another. For the United States, while among the sovereign nations, e. g., exercising sovereign functions for the people—and this is all the major premise means—do not partake of all the attributes of sovereignty which those nations possess of which as a class the United States are a member; nor yet of those attributes by which banks may be chartered. Sovereignty may be limited or plenary. Russia is a sovereignty in which the Czar is the source of law bound by no limitation whatever; England is a sovereignty bound by a vague constitution known as the ethical law; Switzerland is a sovereignty bound by a written constitution of the utmost strictness. Therefore, although all are sovereign, some things can be predicated of Russia that cannot be predicated of England. Some things are possible to England which are impossible to Switzerland. As Mr. Lawrence points out in his essays: "All sovereign states are equal before the law, although some may be more powerful and influential than others."[20] Any state is sovereign which is self-existent, which commands authority in civil society, which directs its citizens and moulds its institutions and which is a member of the family of nations. But it is a clear fallacy to use the term sovereignty in connection with those nations which have all power on all subjects and then use it in application to a nation which by its organic law has all power on a few subjects, and those to be constitutionally exercised, and no power whatever on a vast number of subjects.

Hamilton started out with this remarkable proposition that the definition of government, and the definition necessary to be used for the United States "essential to every step of its progress is that it is sovereign." Government may be an entity produced by compact; but that the definition of government is that it is sovereign is certainly novel. It would be just as scientific to say that the definition of government is that it is a democracy or an oligarchy. Sovereignty is an attribute or a quality, and does not comprehend the thing known as government. And if Hamilton meant to say that the United States were sovereign as much as any nation, he knew that the definition was untenable, because he knew that no government is sovereign in the sense in which he used the term which is limited in its operation by its charter of creation proceeding from its creators and enumerating its powers and limitations. While all nations possess sovereign powers, while all are on an equality with each other before the law of nations, they are sovereign in different degrees, in the same manner that all men possess strength, but are not all equally strong. And while Hamilton was reasoning from analogy it was necessary for him to keep in mind the principle that the United States might resemble all other nations in the quality of sovereignty without at all resembling them in the quantity of sovereignty. Analogy does not imply a resemblance of one thing to another, but only the resemblance of relations. Thus the Czar of Russia and the President of the United States are both executive officers, but it by no means follows that because they resemble each other in being executive officers that there is a resemblance between the things themselves. For instance, who would pretend that the president is an executive and can make a law because the Czar is an executive and can make a law?

Hence Hamilton's next premise that every power vested in every government is sovereign is a *non sequitur*, because it might be admitted without conceding that the United States are sovereign in the sense in which he used the term. In other words, the United States might have sovereign powers without the United States being a sovereign power in the sense that Russia is a sovereign power. Then as a conclusion he insisted that the term sovereign included a right to employ all the means requisite and fairly applicable to the attainments of the ends of such power. Given a sovereign power the designated means could be used to attain the ends of such power. To make his argument more concrete, the constitution empowers congress "to provide and maintain a navy." That being a sovereign power, not because the constitution vests the power, but because "every power vested in the government is sovereign," as he argued, any means "requisite and fairly applicable" might be used to attain it, while the constitution says that the means must be "necessary and proper." He simply ignored the language of the constitution and asserted that those means could be used which the constitution does not permit. It was incumbent upon Hamilton to prove that the United States had the particular power to incorporate a bank, whereas, his deduction based upon the premise that any sovereign nation could incorporate a bank contained a formal fallacy, because his terms were not distributed so as to make that capable of being affirmed of the United States which he affirmed of any sovereign nation.

To what point now does Hamilton's argument conduct us? First, that the definition of every government is that it is sovereign; second, every power vested in every government is sovereign; third, the term sovereign includes the right to employ all the means requisite and fairly applicable to the attainment of the ends of such power.

It would seem that if every government is sovereign it is mere tautology calculated to confuse the subject to say that every power vested in a sovereign government is sovereign. It is not necessary to predicate of a sovereign government that its powers are sovereign. If the government is sovereign it is either so with reference to a few subjects or as to all subjects. Which sort of sovereignty do the United States possess? If they have sovereignty only as to a few subjects, the particular legislation must come within the scope of the subjects; if they have sovereignty as to all subjects the argument is at once closed and elaborate metaphysics is unnecessary to establish that which every man of sound mind must perceive to be within the principle of inclusion. If congress is an English parliament, holding within itself all power because in theory all the people of the nation are in the chamber where it sits, the incorporation of a bank is but a trifling exercise of the plenary commission. If congress is a body representing the people only so far as the constitution defines and permits, the incorporation of a bank must be brought within the scope of the constitution. The sovereignty of the United States has nothing to do with the question, except in so far as sovereignty has been granted and that must include the power necessary to use.

But Hamilton's three terms did not exhaust his doubts and scruples. He conceded that all means requisite and fairly applicable could be used which

(a) Are not precluded by restrictions and exceptions specified in the constitution.

(b) Not immoral.

(c) Not contrary to the essential ends of political society.

Why make these exceptions? They convert the whole argument into a sophistical jumble. If he had adhered to his original terms and predicated sovereignty of the United States and then predicated of that sovereignty every attribute possessed by any nation he might have had a homogeneous argument. If, on the other hand, he wanted to make a constitutional argument, he was familiar enough with the subject from personal contact to have interpreted it along the line necessary to its perversion. But in welding the two arguments together he produced a result which dissolves under analysis.

His first qualification that any means may be used, not precluded by restrictions and exceptions in the constitution is a baseless assumption, which has been repudiated by every constitutional interpreter of any note. We have already shown that several of the states in their instruments of ratification requested an amendment in the constitution which should declare that all powers not delegated by the states or the people were reserved. Hamilton was a member of the New York convention and that state demanded the amendment. Marshall was a member of the Virginia convention and Virginia demanded the amendment. Massachusetts, New Hampshire, Rhode Island and South Carolina demanded the amendment. And the amendment was proposed by the first congress and afterwards adopted by all the states in which it was declared that "the powers not delegated to the United States by the constitution nor prohibited by it to the states are reserved to the states respectively or to the people."

This amendment covered in terms the doctrine of enumeration; for as Lord Bacon[21] said enumeration weakens law in cases not enumerated. Under the Baconian rule, if a power was not mentioned among a list of powers enumerated, it was excluded as a matter of construction; which does not take into account the fact that the constitution proceeded from the people, and as Marshall said in the Virginia convention: "Does not a power remain until it is given away?"

Hamilton's dictum that all means could be used to an end not precluded by restrictions and exceptions was a statement of revolution and nothing less. It followed from that that congress was a British parliament, except where it was restrained by exceptions and restrictions. For, while the British parliament is the sole repository of power, the English constitution, consisting of the ethical law, operates as a restrictive influence upon legislative action. No one was ever bold enough to affirm this proposition since Hamilton's day until the author of the Insular decisions revamped it.[22] But Hamilton further argued that in spite of sovereignty and sovereign powers, that no means could be used which were immoral. It is very difficult to understand why immoral means could not be used. The constitution permits "necessary and proper" means, and many means might be necessary to sovereign power which would be at the same time immoral. Sovereign nations habitually use the most immoral means for ends alleged to be necessary and moral, and for ends understood to be immoral. Mr. Story defined sovereignty to be "supreme, absolute, uncontrollable power, the *jus summi imperii*, the absolute right to govern." So that, if the right is based upon sovereignty its morality need not be urged. It is inconsequential and beside the point.

Let each man bring it home to himself acting as a champion for a commercial monopoly, and on the question of its lawful creation, imagine himself volunteering the question of its morality. It must be conceded that Hamilton's audacity was satanic. For in his report on the bank he had provided "No similar institution shall be established by any future act of the United States, during the continuance of the one hereby proposed to be established."[23] This he knew; this he had written. And he knew the horror with which the people of the day regarded monopolies, and that his own state of New York in its convention of adoption of which he was a member, had recommended as an amendment to the constitution "that congress do not grant monopolies." The amendment was not proposed by congress because the tenth and eleventh amendments covered that point, and were understood to cover it.

But in spite of the sovereignty of the United States if congress could adopt no immoral means to an end, how could the bank be justified? It was a monopoly and intended by Hamilton to be such. A monopoly is essentially immoral. It strikes down equal rights; it grants special privileges; it destroys instead of preserving the "blessings of liberty;" it extorts tribute without any equivalent in return; it exacts servitude, and it breeds hatred and disorder in the state. Such has been the history of monopolies; while their evil influences have so menaced the absolutism of thrones that despots have been forced to control them and in some instances to eradicate them. Hamilton's exception based upon the morality of means, related as it was to the consideration of a commercial monopoly, was a piece of sardonic irony which entitles him to a place beside Richelieu and Lord Bacon.[24]

Hamilton's third exception to the use of all means excludes all those which might be contrary to the essential ends of political society. He does not explain what are the essential ends of political society. But if a monopoly was not in his judgment contrary to those essential ends, it is possible that in his judgment many other institutions, such as nobility, mortmain[25] or state religion might not be contrary to such ends. Whatever the ends of political society are in the abstract or in general, the ends of the political society known as the United States are set forth in the preamble of their constitution. The government was ordained "to establish justice," and if so not to deny it by the creation of monopolies: "to insure domestic tranquillity," and therefore not to foment hatred and discord among the people by the abuse of government in the enactment of partial and oppressive laws; "to promote the general welfare," and, therefore, not to promote the particular welfare of a few at the expense of the many; "to secure the blessings of liberty to ourselves and our posterity,"' and, therefore, not to detract from the rights of some to add to the advantages of others and thereby to invade the liberty declared to be an object of regard.

Hamilton then proceeded to other enunciations. If, he argued, the United States are not less sovereign, as to "proper objects," because the states are sovereign as to their "proper objects;" if laws made in "pursuance of the constitution," are the supreme law of the land—then "the power which can create the supreme law of the land in any case, is doubtless sovereign as to such case."[26] How does this follow? He has affirmed that the United States are sovereign as to their "proper objects;" then that laws made in "pursuance of the constitution" are the supreme law of the land. Then the ground is shifted. The succeeding proposition is that "the power" can create the supreme law "in any case," whether "in pursuance of the constitution" or not, whether as to "proper objects" or not. And therefore, the power which can create the supreme law in "any case" is obviously sovereign "as to such case." It is more; it is sovereign as to every case! And what is in fact proven with respect to the United States?

From so many postulates he deduced the following: "This general and indisputable principle (e. g., creating the supreme law of the land) puts at once an end to the abstract question whether the United States have power to erect a corporation." For "It is unquestionably incident to sovereign power to erect corporations and consequently to that of the United States in relation to the objects entrusted to the management of the government."

Creating the supreme law of the land in every case, or to be more specific, creating a corporation as incident to the power of creating the supreme law of the land, is a different thing from passing a law in pursuance of the constitution. For if it be not in pursuance of the constitution, it is not the supreme law of the land; it is not law at all. How, then, is the question of creating a corporation put at rest by asserting that laws passed in pursuance of the constitution are supreme? Here is a clear *petitio principii*.[27] The main thing remains to be proven, namely, that a law chartering a bank is in pursuance of the constitution and therefore is a law, and as to all the sovereignties known as the States is supreme. Nor is the power to charter corporations an incident of sovereignty, except as the term sovereignty means supreme, absolute, uncontrollable power, which the United States were not alleged to possess. Such power would be an incident, that is to say, inhering in or attached to an uncontrollable, absolute power. But when uncontrollable, absolute power is denied by express constitutional provisions It is incumbent upon him who has the affirmative to prove that the particular incidents of sovereignty are attached to some sovereign agency or commission expressed in the constitution.

Hamilton's argument then reduces itself to these assertions:

(a) Every government is sovereign;

(b) Every power vested in a sovereign government is sovereign;

(c) A government to effectuate any sovereign power may use any means;

(1) Not precluded or excepted;

(2) Not immoral;

(3) Not contrary to the essential ends of political society;

(d) The United States are sovereign because the constitution and laws passed in pursuance thereof are supreme;

(e) Therefore the United States may charter corporations;

This is the lauded foundation upon which American absolutism rests, for it is absolutism and nothing else. It is a sheer waste of time to argue that a law is not necessary or proper, because if the republic was constructed to rest upon a question of etymology it was doomed from the day of the adoption of the constitution. The question of the bank was argued at length upon the definition of the word "necessary," and Hamilton, with labored logic, connected the necessity of the bank with the express power of borrowing money, raising revenue and equipping armies. The word necessary imports inevitability both in its radical and its popular significance. But the word has synonyms of lesser shades of meaning which Hamilton contended should be used in construing the "sweeping clause." On this branch of the question he sophisticated[28] the constitution to empower congress to incorporate the bank. Not satisfied wholly with his own argument for this source of power, nor for the source of the power in the sovereignty of the United States, he dwelt upon the territorial clause wherein the congress is given power to make all needful rules and regulations for the territory or other property of the United States which he said included the power to erect municipal or public corporations. Therefore, he said, the power to erect a corporation of the highest nature was granted by the constitution; and a bank might be incorporated under the clause giving the congress power to make all needful rules and regulations respecting the territory or other property of the United States. Because, he argued, money is property and "therefore the money to be raised by taxes as well as any other personal property must be supposed to come within the meaning as they certainly do within the letter of authority to make all needful rules and regulations concerning the property of the United States." And hence the bank might be an institution connected with the property of the United States which they are empowered to control by all needful rules and regulations. This branch of the argument does not rise to the dignity of a question, nor ought serious discussion to be provoked by the claim that a money monopoly is necessary to the execution of any enumerated power of congress.

But because the argument upon the sovereignty of the United States is the real strength of imperialism and of the rapidly centralizing tendencies of the government the specious bubble should be exploded. That as an implication of sovereignty the United States may adopt colonialism and as a corollary maintain under the control of the president an army in distant islands or in any part of the world is one of the flimsiest political pretenses ever made. What is the meaning of the historic and settled principle that the federal constitution is a grant of power? Manifestly that a residue remains in the grantor and that the power not granted remains with the sovereignty which made the grant, namely, the states or the people through the states. Or what is meant by the correlative of this principle that the state constitutions are a limitation upon power? Manifestly that ultimate sovereignty or paramount and absolute power is with the people who are the source of all authority in this land. For power here proceeds from the people up, and not as in monarchies from the sovereign down. Now suppose neither the states nor the people want a policy pursued; yet what can prevent it if the United States are the sovereign power, the repository of sovereign power, of paramount power, and their officials construe the sovereign power to the support of the unwelcome policy? Is it any answer to say that the people at the polls can reject or confirm the policy? No man who loves or understands constitutional government will say so. Nor can it be maintained for a moment that sovereignty is in the United States. Chief Justice Marshall in the great case of Gibbons v. Ogden said: "It has been said that they (the states under the Confederacy) were sovereign, were completely independent and were connected with each other only by a league. This is true."[29] Now when the constitution was framed they withdrew from the confederacy and formed "a more perfect union" under the constitution, as its preamble declares. But while they gave it into the hands of the general government to exercise great sovereign powers, they did not surrender their sovereignty, nor did the people back of the states surrender to any entity their paramount power. As laid down by Vattel[30] nothing can be implied to increase the grant of power of the sovereign. The powers granted in the constitution to the United States are incidents of sovereignty, e. g., to declare war, coin money, lay taxes. But as the great constitutional lawyers of the past so often pointed out how absurd to specify and grant these incidents of sovereignty if sovereignty itself in its entirety was by the constitution transferred from the states and from the people, and at once by the ratification of the constitution vested in the general government with all the plenitude of its power. If the United States are sovereign, as the imperialists use the term, how is the constitution a grant of power; why were amendments to the constitution contemplated, and why should they be ratified by three-fourths of the several states? How can this monstrous sophistry of Hamilton, grown into imperialism itself, consist with the tenth amendment that "powers not delegated to the United States by the constitution nor prohibited by it (the constitution) to the states are reserved to the states respectively or to the people?" Powers of sovereignty the United States have had from the beginning, and should have had; but they never had sovereignty, because it was never granted to them, and at the time of the adoption of the constitution it was in the states or the people of the states, as we may choose to view the question.

The doctrine of implied powers being sophistical in itself conducts to still more startling fallacies. For instance, it is an incident of sovereignty to make war, but by implication do the United States possess in connection with that incident of sovereignty the power of a sovereign nation to annex distant territory and overwhelm the order and the liberty of the states which granted the incident of sovereignty to make war? If so constitutions are superfluous, because language is not exact enough to express the limitations intended to be imposed. They can be avoided and evaded and the whole sovereignty drawn over to the medium of sovereignty by the deductions of metaphysics. How nearly shall be realized the prophesy of George Mason contained in the objections to the constitution which he submitted to the Virginia legislature? In explaining his refusal to sign the constitution he said: "The judiciary of the United States is so constructed and extended as to absorb and destroy the judiciary of the several states, thereby rendering laws as tedious, intricate and expensive and justice as unattainable by a great part of the community as in England; and enabling the rich to oppress and ruin the poor. * * * This government will commence in a moderate aristocracy; it is at present impossible to see whether it will in its operations produce a monarchy or a corrupt, offensive aristocracy. It will most probably vibrate some years between the two and then terminate in the one or the other."

An army fighting for liberty at home, and an army fighting against liberty abroad is the measure of constitutional progression which gives truth to these words. The cautious ninth and tenth amendments have turned out to be of no binding consequence? For, as seen, although the constitution is a grant of power; although enumeration of powers shall not be construed to deny or disparage those retained by the people; although powers not delegated are retained by the people—a system of legal sophistry, devised in large part by Hamilton and perfected by his followers, has sufficed to incorporate companies, confer special privileges and ingraft the very substance of monarchy upon the republic in the form of colonialism. What could the general government have done in addition if the people in the states had surrendered to it all power whatsoever? This denouement would be ridiculous if the ultimate scene already foreshadowed did not give promise of one of the most deplorable declines recorded in history.

This, then, is the foundation upon which rests the whole superstructure of that alleged sovereignty which never existed in the constitution. As it was cemented with a mixture of falsehood and fraud it is doomed to dissolve in the process of time which eats away all that is unreal; but when the foundation falls will not all that was good in our system perish with all of this created evil? What providence will reverse the universal rule?

Notes

1. For further information on the American Revolution, see Robert Middlekauff, *The Glorious Cause: The American Revolution, 1763–1789* (New York: Oxford University Press, 2007).

2. "Fundamental law or constitution of a state or nation." Henry Campbell Black, *A Dictionary of Law* (St. Paul, MN: West Publishing Co., 1891), 856.

3. "Rapidity of motion; swiftness; speed." *Webster's Practical Dictionary*, s.v. "celerity."

4. Baron de Montesquieu, French political philosopher, whose influential work *The Spirit of Laws* (1750) established the principles of the separation of governmental powers (legislative, executive, and judicial). See Robert Shackleton, *Montesquieu: A Critical Biography* (London: Oxford University Press, 1961).

5. For a general overview of the Constitution of 1787, constitutionalism, and the Constitutional Convention, see Carol Berkin, *A Brilliant Solution: Inventing the American Constitution* (New York: Harcourt, 2002).

6. Article (No.) 44 of "The Federalist Papers" was written by Madison and appeared originally in the *New York Packet* on January 25, 1788. See Albert Furtwangler, *The Authority of Publius: A Reading of the Federalist Papers* (Ithaca: Cornell University Press, 1984).

7. A law which deals with acts done before its passage. *Webster's Practical Dictionary*, s.v. "ex post facto."

8. Articles of Confederation, Article II.

9. U.S. Constitution, Article I, Section 8, clause 18.

10. Jonathan Elliot, ed., *The Debates in the Several State Conventions on the Adoption of the Federal Constitution as Recommended by the General Convention at Philadelphia*

in 1787 . . . , 2nd ed., 5 vols. (Washington, D.C.: Taylor and Maury, 1836–59), 1:147. Masters relied heavily on this work, and unless otherwise noted, all subsequent quotations for the remainder of this chapter are drawn from Elliot's editions.

11. See note 6 above for further information on the Federalist Papers.

12. Masters likely intended the asterisks in this essay to function like ellipses.

13. Alexander Hamilton, "The Federalist Papers," No. 33.

14. Timothy Walker, *Introduction to American Law: Designed as a First Book for Students*, 6th ed. (Boston: Little, Brown, 1874), 185. Masters rearranges this quote. The original reads, "It purports to be an additional power, and not a restriction; to enlarge, and not to diminish the powers of Congress."

15. "Extending to a great length; indulging in protracted discourse; long; diffuse; tedious; tiresome; wearisome." *Webster's Practical Dictionary*, s.v. "prolix."

16. "One who governs alone; an aristocrat; a monarch." *Webster's Complete Dictionary of the English Language* (London: George Bell and Sons, 1886), s.v. "monocrat."

17. U.S. Constitution, Preamble to the Bill of Rights; Amendment IX; Amendment X.

18. For further general information on the debates surrounding the creation of a United States bank, see Gordon S. Wood, *Empire of Liberty: A History of the Early Republic, 1789–1815* (Oxford: Oxford University Press, 2009).

19. Like the debates surrounding the adoption of the Constitution, Masters is drawing on Elliot's *Debates* as his source material unless otherwise noted. See note 10 above.

20. Masters is referring to T. J. Lawrence (1849–1920), a prominent professor of international law. Though the direct quote could not be traced, Lawrence makes similar statements in several of his works, including *A Handbook of Public International Law* (London: George Bell and Sons, 1890), 33; *Essays on Some Disputed Questions in Modern International Law* (London: George Bell and Sons, 1884), 14; and *The Principles of International Law* (Boston: D. C. Heath, 1895), 67.

21. Francis Bacon (1561–1626), lawyer, statesman, and lord chancellor of England famous for his scientific, literary, and juridical works.

22. Also known as the Insular Cases; series of opinions issued by the U.S. Supreme Court in 1901 that served to allow the U.S. Congress to administer territories acquired by the United States in the Spanish-American War. Juan R. Torruella, "Ruling America's Colonies: The Insular Cases," *Yale Law Review* 32, no. 1 (2013): 58.

23. Alexander Hamilton, "Final Version of the Second Report on the Further Provision Necessary for Establishing Public Credit (Report on a National Bank), 13 December 1790," *Founders Online*, National Archives, https://founders.archives.gov/documents/Hamilton/01-07-02-0229-0003 [accessed March 7, 2022].

24. Armand-Jean du Plessis, cardinal et duc de Richelieu (1585–1642), chief minister to Louis XIII of France, infamous for his support of royal absolutism and political machinations, and immortalized in Victor Hugo's *The Three Musketeers*. See note 21 above for information on Lord Bacon.

25. "Possession of lands to tenements in dead hands, or hands that cannot alienate, orig. by the church, now by any corporation." *Webster's Practical Dictionary*, s.v. "mortmain."

26. The quotes from this paragraph and subsequent paragraphs come from Alexander Hamilton, "Hamilton's Opinion as to the Constitutionality of the Bank of the United States," in *The Federalist: A Commentary on the Constitution of the United States by Alexander Hamilton, James Madison, and John Jay*, ed. Paul Leicester Ford (New York: Henry Holt, 1898), 655–78.

27. "The assumption of truth without cause," Black, *Dictionary*, 896.

28. "To render worthless by admixture; to pervert, adulterate, debase, corrupt, vitiate." *Webster's Practical Dictionary*, s.v. "sophisticate."

29. *Gibbons v. Ogden* (1824) was a U.S. Supreme Court case establishing that Congress, not the individual states, has the power to regulate interstate commerce, leading to the breakup of navigation monopolies. This quote is from the opinion written by Chief Justice John Marshall. See Thomas Cox, *Gibbons V. Ogden, Law, and Society in the Early Republic* (Athens, OH: Ohio University Press, 2009).

30. Emmerich de Vattel (1714–67), Swiss jurist and author of *The Law of Nations* (1758), an influential treatise on the application of natural law theory to international relations.

ELECT THE
FEDERAL JUDGES

O NE of the great political parties has already taken a conventional stand in favor of electing senators by a direct vote of the people. This question when recently brought to an acute point of discussion was met by Senator Lodge[1] of Massachusetts by an astonishing objection. It was that the election of senators by the people would destroy the constitutional theory of senators as representing states. The essence of his objection, if he were correctly reported, consisted in regarding the senators as "Ambassadors of the states," which their popular election would un-character. It cannot be perceived how the manner of their election by a state would make them less the representatives of the state as such. But this objection made by an exponent of the school which has taught that the constitution was the product of the people of America, and not the people of the states of America seems incongruous.

A reform of equal, if not indeed of deeper moment, is the election of the members of the Federal judiciary for terms of moderate length. The reasons which were urged in favor of a Federal judiciary appointed for life were long ago discovered to be pretentious and unsound. The Federal courts have for so long a time pursued a course of systematic usurpation that doubt can no longer be maintained against the accumulating proof that these tribunals are today among the greatest enemies of justice and liberty.

Hamilton, in the 78th number of the Federalist made an examination of the constitutional provision for the Federal judiciary.[2] He concluded that the judiciary was the weakest department of the government because it held neither the purse nor the sword; that it had neither force nor will, but merely judgment; that it could never attack the executive or legislative branches of the government; that the general liberty of the people could never be endangered by the judiciary. These are very sweeping declarations, which their author was content to express without demonstration of any sort. To what extent need they be respected? The Supreme Court may validate or invalidate revenue laws. Through custom and according to the suppositious logic of the constitution, as maintained by Hamilton himself in the Federalist, the Supreme Court has the power to construe the constitution with reference to any particular law, and to hold the latter void if repugnant to the constitution. But whether the law is so repugnant rests in the judgment of the Supreme Court to decide; and therefore, what that court says the constitution imports is the ultimate and unappealable formation of the constitution itself. Construction, therefore, of the constitution relating to appropriations relates to the purse itself, to which extent the court does hold the purse. While the court has altogether successfully protected what Hamilton called the property of the country. The inferior Federal courts may, and repeatedly have, done the same thing. And this is in no artificial sense a holding of the purse also.

The legislative and executive branches of the government are attacked when the court overthrows legislation which those branches have enacted. Their powers are utterly prostrated when they can no longer perform their functions. They are subdued to the "force and will" of another mind when what they choose to call the law is declared by the Supreme Court to be void and no law. The general liberty of the people is not only endangered but infringed upon by this course; and as historic fact this has occurred repeatedly. A system which begets in the popular mind, and to a degree in the legislative mind, the idea that a judgment of the Supreme Court between private parties is a rule of political action to which the country must settle down to tolerate, is pernicious beyond expression. So much nevertheless for theory respecting the character of these courts. It is proper to refer to Hamilton's arguments in the Federalist upon these subjects because they were addressed to the people of the United States at a time when grave doubts were entertained of certain features of the constitution which these arguments had a tendency to quiet. And because since his day nothing further of moment has been advanced in favor of the appointment of Federal judges for life.

Experience has demonstrated that the theory is wrong. The Federal courts today have few friends among impartial thinkers familiar with their practices; and abhorrence of them as the merciless and willing tools of special privilege is fast gaining ground.

Hamilton thought the people should have no voice in the making of Federal judges. If this matter should be committed to the people "there would be too great a disposition to consult popularity, to justify a reliance that nothing would be consulted but the constitution and the laws."[3] Let us see, then, what power outside of people can create these judges. The president, according to the original theory, was to be elected by electors, the latter being generally chosen by the legislators. Now the legislators have always been chosen by popular vote, and so their temper and character depend upon the people from whom in fact they come. The electors were taken from the body of the people by the legislature, and these chose the president. How is it then that men competent to choose those upon whose choice depends the president, who appoints the judges, cannot directly choose the judges themselves? In the choice of judges, what indeed becomes of those select bodies known as the legislatures and the electoral college which, though of aristocratical standing, for the purpose of selecting the executive, have no will in the matter of selecting the judges? As to the senators, they are the creatures of legislatures which are the creatures of the people. It is a fallacious doctrine which attributes more rightful power to agents than the principals are alleged themselves to possess. The scheme of appointment of Federal judges by the president and the senate is conceived in distrust of human nature; and yet neither the president nor the senate is distrusted in the selection, and the judges when once installed are trusted to the utmost limit upon the ground that they need not reckon with the passions of the populace. The Federal courts are

the fit product of such reasoning as this. As they are placed beyond
the reach of the people they may successfully despise the wishes of
the people both when they run counter to and when they run parallel
with the constitution itself. They are the creatures of plutocracy and
with few exceptions uniformly obey its mandates. So far then from
being that body of ideal independence which a dissembling doctrine
has made them out they have been slavishly attentive not to popular
rights but to special privilege. It has been said that these courts follow
the election returns, and if so the manner of their appointment and the
tenure of their office have not made them independent. If so they do
sometimes consult popularity instead of the constitution. But deeper
consideration of the question will show that they do not always bow
to the paramount party and that their apparent regard for the popular
will is generally a regard for the will of plutocracy.

The judiciary so far as points of comparison exist is the strongest
branch of the government. While the legislative power is in abeyance
at intervals the judicial power never sleeps. It continues to accumulate
the *lex non scripta,* by applying its own reason to facts as they come up
and by filling up the interstices of the constitution with cement from the
Bastile and the Tower.[4] It may furnish laws for the executive to faithfully
execute by issuing injunctions which the military may be called on to
enforce. Thus the judges in no unscientific sense make the law. A line is
drawn between making and interpreting the law; and while courts may
not make the law they declare it. But before the law can be declared it
must be ascertained, and its ascertainment involves a strong admixture
of legislative action. Thus, to say that the judicial department is the
weakest branch of the government, that it only interprets the law and
does not make the law, is a plain overlooking of practical experience.
That the judiciary should be created to be and to remain independent
is well enough. But to make the judges independent of the people is
something else. There is such a contrast between the refined idealism
of the constitutional construction of the judiciary and the sordid use
to which it has put itself that the suggestion is inevitable to give this
human institution a human birth. The people have the practical and
philosophic right to directly elect Federal judges, because they interpret
and practically enact a large body of the laws which determine the

rights and remedies of the people. The world has grown too practical to longer believe that any divinity hedges the judicial department of either the state or the Federal government. We are too far distant from the time when judges were the vicegerents of the royal personage to be much affected by the attempt to perpetuate the atmosphere of royalty. There is no more reason for the judiciary to be independent than for the legislature or the executive to be independent; and there is no more reason to make it independent by appointing the judges for life than to make the executive or the Congress independent by appointing the executive or the Congress for life. The three departments of the government stand on a precise equality with reference to the end to be attained, and the means to attain those ends. The end of legitimate government is the establishment of justice. In the last analysis this depends upon the individual moral man. The fact that the man is independent of the people does not make him moral. If, when he becomes a judge he is moral he may become unjust by insidious influences and by a sense of absolute power, which make resistance to such influences unnecessary, except for the integrity of his own mind, an ideal not always strong enough for the purpose. The fact, however, that the man is made a judge by the people does not make him moral. In the latter case, though, if he turns out to be an enemy of liberty, the people have the remedy of putting him out of power, so that he may not be for his whole life an instrument of evil and tyranny. An elective judiciary which submits to popular impulse (e. g., which in doing so violates the law of justice) is no worse than a president or Congress which does so. The results are no more disastrous. Where the power is in the people to speedily correct their mistakes they may and frequently do correct them. Where mistakes are made by an absolute department of the government there is no remedy except that slow reformation in which either the excitative occasion of the evil passes away, or in which the minds of the wrong-doers become amenable to better influences or new powers take the place of the old. The truth is, however, that so-called popular impulse is neither so frequent nor so dangerous as anti-republican alarmists have made out. It is not so much to be feared or warded against as those studied and incessant machinations done in secret against justice and liberty by those who wish an absolute judiciary to keep down great reactions of the people produced by wrongs long endured. Whatever makes for injustice, whether through popular impulse or through secret encroachment, should be avoided. But it is an unphilosophic if not dishonest system, which so far takes account of popular impulse as to give secret encroachment the absolute mastery of the situation. Whether for good or for evil the people have the undoubted right to directly control the selection of the Federal judges, both for the supreme and inferior courts. This is not the same thing as the rule of the majority right or wrong; but if it were, the principle which justifies popular control as to any branch of the government from the necessity of the case justifies it as to all departments. There is no higher rightful power than the people in this or any other government. A few men who have become empowered to create the incumbents of one department of the people's government, will not be attentive to the general interest in their selections. Each appointment of a Federal judge has shown that the questions considered were politics, and the influence of railroads or other corporations. Men of learning and ability have not been appointed because they were men of learning or ability, but because first and chiefly they have leaned toward special privilege or that economic philosophy which unjustly distributes the wealth of the country, or seeks to keep it so distributed. The independence which the Federal judiciaries have manifested is a mere absolutism in favor of plutocracy, with a fearless disregard of what the people think or desire. They have shown no greater judicial ability than the state judges, outside of a few distinguished exceptions; while their stability has consisted in adhering to the interests of their creators in further consideration of distinguished favors and social attentions from those who control the wealth of the land. If the Supreme Court or the inferior Federal Courts may invalidate an act of Congress, a state constitution or a state law, or if it may, as recently suggested, even assume to invalidate an amendment to the Federal Constitution itself because not constitutionally passed, it follows that it is the ultimate and most powerful body in the structure of our government, and that its members ought either to be elected by the people for terms of moderate length, say six years, or else it should be deprived of the power to sit in judgment upon the validity of these acts of the people. The danger to free institutions from these extraordinary powers cannot otherwise be avoided. It is a novel system under which the people may exert their whole energies to place in power a Congress to pass a particular law conceived by the people to be needful, only to have the law when passed set aside by the vote of one man, that is, by a vote of five to four in the court. And it is the more novel when it is considered that the people who ratified the Federal Constitution did not directly confer the power. It has been derived through the adjudication of the very court which exercises it. The necessity for the power was determined by the court which uses the power. Thus, to determine the necessity for the power to be in the court, which so determines and uses the power, and to use it to overthrow the legislative will are not acts of the weakest branch of the government. In theory the Constitution is the direct expression of the people themselves and an act of Congress is the representative expression of the people. But the sequence to these propositions is not that the Supreme Court may authoritatively say when the law conforms to and when it conflicts with the Constitution. That power ought to be expressly conferred upon the court to be exercised by it, and not metaphysically deduced by the court, which assumes this supreme function.

Even the interpretation of the law does not extend to the invalidation of the law. The court could give its opinion that the law is unconstitutional, as the attorney general frequently does, and this would be interpretation. The Congress very frequently considers the constitutionality of proposed legislation before passing upon it, and this is interpretation. The English courts interpret the law, but they may not invalidate an Act of Parliament. The invalidation of an act of congress is something more than interpretation; it is the binding judgment following interpretation. What would have been the consequence if the Supreme Court at the beginning had adopted the practice of giving its interpretation instead of its judgment upon the theory that the several branches of the government arc independent, and that it is no more the guardian of the Constitution than either of the other branches? Manifestly in due season the sober intellect of the country would have enforced the repeal of unconstitutional legislation; or if not, would the final result have been worse than the revolutionary judgments which the Supreme Court has rendered at intervals of time, such as

McCulloch vs. Maryland and Downes vs. Bidwell?[5] Have not the bulk of these decisions, which invalidated national laws, state laws and municipal ordinances, led straight to the intrenchment of special privilege? Have not the several clauses of the Constitution restraining state action been construed to cripple the people in their defence against organized wealth? If the Supreme Court judges had been responsible to the people at large every six years would they have been favorable to special interests? Out of the historic origin of courts as the emanations of royal authority, out of the maxim that courts interpret the law, out of the axiom that a lower law is less law than a higher law has grown the dangerous system that the Supreme Court ought to be independent of the people and revered as a sacred fountain of authority, and may solely adjudge the invalidity of a law; and that such a judgment even in a suit between private parties becomes a rule of political action. A people which pretends to be free and self-governing may well wake up to the necessity, and for these reasons alone, of placing the Federal judiciaries, both supreme and inferior, under popular control.

But, perhaps the most fruitful source of jurisdiction for the Federal Courts arises out of the enlargement of controversies between citizens of different states. Corporations, when in a confidential mood, make the boast that the Federal Courts always have and always will take care of the property of the country, which means the people who have property. Specific data could be obtained of the cases lost and won by the railroads which remove their cases to the Federal Courts in Chicago. But it may be sufficient to say that the attorney of one of these railroads recently stated that he had never lost a case for his company in these courts. Federal judges take a specific oath to do justice between the rich and the poor alike, and it is not perceived what claim property as such can legitimately make upon the attention of these courts. But it is a notorious fact that the jurisdiction of the state courts are set aside by the removal acts and all corporations, which can use the Federal jurisdictions. The Constitution itself provides that the Federal Courts shall have jurisdiction of controversies between citizens of different states. For the purposes of removal corporations are held to be citizens of the state of their creation, because conclusively presumed to be composed of citizens of that state, and these removals have been and often are made in the face of facts which overcame that presumption if it ever should have obtained.

Thus, a number of men residing in Chicago, and who are citizens of Illinois, procure the incorporation of a company under the laws of New Jersey. These men own the stock of the company, the business property may all be located in Illinois. These men demand the protecting powers of the state authorities for their New Jersey company. Yet, if the company is sued in the courts of Illinois, by a citizen of Illinois, the company removes the cause to the Federal Court on the ground that there is a controversy between citizens of different states. The point is, a corporation is not a citizen. A citizen is a person. For a corporation is an artificial body, and a modem corporation is not the persons who procure the charter. They are not empowered as incorporators and their successors to exercise certain chartered powers. The theory of controversies between citizens of different states, entitling the Federal Courts to take jurisdiction, is exceedingly simple. As the states were independent republics it was naturally supposed that there might be local prejudice against a citizen of a different state, who should come or be brought in a state court; and that a citizen of the state in which the suit was brought would have an advantage over the citizen of another state in the local courts. The Federal Courts being inter-state tribunals, were thought to be the safest forums for the adjustment of controversies between citizens of different states. But how is there a controversy between such citizens when the chief, if not all the parties in interest in a New Jersey corporation, are citizens of Illinois, and the adverse party to the suit is a citizen of Illinois? Thus, such a New Jersey corporation can, under the system which has grown up, try its suits in the Federal Courts in every state in the Union, except New Jersey. As all the great corporations are chartered in some one of these states which has recognized the "logic of monopoly," it follows that they are independent of the state laws and the state courts. All the great railroads and all the great corporations thus seek the shelter of the Federal Courts whose independence from popular passions makes the law sure and smooth for them. It is a notorious fact, too, that the rules of the Federal Courts are so drawn that the poor have the barest chance of success. The way is bestrewn with complex technicalities, with arbitrary rulings. There is not, in fact, the right of trial by jury in these courts; there is only the favor of such a trial upon the consent of the judge. For the judge can withdraw any case from the jury, and the practice of doing so is notoriously common. The court passes on the facts, the court instructs the jury orally, and sums up the facts, emphasizing what it chooses. If the jury returns a verdict for a poor man, the court may set it aside. And if this is done the expense and labor of another trial are peculiarly heavy. If one is rendered for a corporation it likely will not be set aside. But if it is, the corporation can serenely await the second trial. The case may be diverted upon some collateral point. A ruling of a court of appeal requires a great deal of money, for the rules of the court impose such onerous burdens upon those who appeal, such as requiring the record to be printed, that appeals are impossible to the poor. Candid consideration of the practice and the rules of these courts will convince any one that they are the courts of plutocracy; and that the poor, the maimed, the oppressed can expect neither pity nor justice in them. Of course, there are exceptions, and exceptional judges. No condemnation upon a subject of this kind can be all inclusive. Also it ought to be said that in a suit between corporations of equal power, between individuals of equal standing, or of equally indifferent standing, or between an individual and an obscure corporation as to some subject not suggestive of the sanctity of property and ordinarily in a criminal cause, a trial in a Federal Court may be fair. Nevertheless, the general condemnation that they are the courts of plutocracy cannot be successfully assailed. What excuse can men have who take a specific oath provided by law to do justice to the rich and the poor alike, so to build up a practice and a jurisprudence that the courts are accessible only to those who have money? The peculiar constitution of the Federal Courts has made this evolution easier than it would have been with them if the judges had been elective. A deep laid plan of imperial consolidation has promoted the enlargement of the jurisdiction of these courts by casuistical reasoning and ill-concealed usurpation until their jurisdiction is practically boundless.

"Depend upon it," wrote Alexander H. Stephens, "there is no difference between consolidation and empire; no difference between centralism and imperialism."[6] When the 14th amendment was added to the Constitution they were poor judges of human nature who supposed that its apparent principles of liberty were in safer hands for being centrally administered than they would have been with the states themselves. And so the brave men who went through the terrible conflict of 1861, and who are yet living, have seen an interpretation put upon its results, which, if anticipated before the war, would have prevented the firing of a shot. A union of men or of states based upon affection is a different thing from a union bound together by force, and whose units are disciplined as to matters of the purest local interest by the appointive judiciary of a consolidated government.

The war abolished the avowed and visible slavery of the negro; but, accurately speaking, what does it amount to in the face of the use to which the 14th amendment has been put?

The 14th amendment is very easily dodged so far as the negro is concerned. And this is done without much objection and generally with applause. While this magna charta[7] of the general government has produced perennial benefits to those whom the abolitionists could scarcely have dreamed would have derived anything out of a glorious war for liberty. The 14th amendment has committed to the care of the Federal Courts every special interest. The states may tax corporations, but the Federal Courts may invalidate the taxation; all sorts of local regulations as to railroads, street railways and what not are invalidated under it. There seems to be no subject of state action which is not covered by the 14th amendment. The result is that the states may do only what the Federal Courts decide the 14th amendment does not prohibit. Philosophically and in truth what was, what could be gained when the power of securing the equal protection of the laws and equal rights for all involved the creation of a virtual empire? What a paradox this is, which purports to secure liberty by destroying the only sources of liberty known then or now, namely, the rule of the people and the supremacy of local government in local affairs. The last few years have seen diabolical constructions placed upon the war of 1861 by the party which claims the glories of that war, and which has been paramount since the war.

If the constitutional sequence of that war is the right to subjugate weaker people and tax them without representation; if as one of its results the military can be supreme at will; if as another of its results the crime of sedition has been created, and freedom of the press and of speech and a right to use the mails have been curtailed or placed at the disposal of the government, then the mere fact that the negro was emancipated in the course of the war does not prevent the conclusion that the deeper impulse projected to this day with studied care was the creation of an empire robed for effect in the apparel of a republic. The Panama episode is good proof that secession of itself is not nearly so reprehensible as the republican party pretended in the days when it inveighed against secession as the embodiment of treason. The powers which have been coaxed from the plausible surface of the 14th amendment, and through which organized wealth has its way in the Federal Courts, is one of the criteria of the meaning of the war of 1861.

The task of taking these courts in hand now devolves upon the people. There is no place in a republic for courts so constituted. Time has fully shown that the reasons advanced in their favor when the constitution was pending before the people were such as men might advance, whose motives were sinister, or such as men might advance from the recesses of the mind, based upon insufficient data and without that experience, which in all matters of policy, is necessary to true knowledge. Jefferson uttered a great truth when he said that better results might be obtained by appointing the judges, but it was doubtful, and in such a case principle should be consulted. The principle was, of course, that the people are the source of government, and necessarily of all of its departments, and that the judges should hold their commissions from the people themselves. Progress points the way to this end. Despotism and retrogression, its accompaniment, look to the perpetuation of the present system.

Notes

1. Henry Cabot Lodge, Republican senator, was a close friend of Theodore Roosevelt and advocate for the annexation of Puerto Rico during the Spanish-American War.

2. No. 78 was written by Hamilton and appeared originally in the *McLean's Edition* on May 28, 1788. See Albert Furtwangler, *The Authority of Publius: A Reading of the Federalist Papers* (Ithaca: Cornell University Press, 1984).

3. Hamilton, *The Federalist No. 78.*

4. Masters is referring to two famous prisons, the Bastille in Paris and the Tower of London. "Lex non scripta" means a law that is not written but is still followed as a law that is written.

5. *McCulloch v. Maryland* (1819) established the constitutionality of the implied powers of the U.S. Congress, meaning that Congress holds the powers expressly outlined in the Constitution, as well as any powers appropriate to facilitate its function. *Downes v. Bidwell* (1901), part of the Insular Cases in the aftermath of the Spanish-American War, determined that Puerto Rico was not part of the United States at its annexation and could be governed directly by Congress under treaty. See Juan R. Torruella, "Ruling America's Colonies: The Insular Cases," *Yale Law Review* 32, no. 1 (2013): 58, 69–70.

6. Alexander H. Stephens (1812–83), governor of Georgia and U.S. senator, most famously the vice president of the Confederate States of America (1861–65). Quotation from Alexander H. Stephens, *A Constitutional View of the Late War between the States; Its Causes, Character, Conduct and Results* (Philadelphia: National Publishing Company, 1870), 2:668.

7. The Magna Charta (or Magna Carta) (1215) resulted from a conflict between King John and the lords of England who sought an articulation of the Crown's power vis-à-vis the aristocracy.

DESPOTISM REVAMPED

T

H E barons of special privilege, all of whom are uniformly supporting the present revolutionary administration,[1] threaten the American people with financial wreckage, unless the policy outlined by the Porto Rican bill[2] shall be approved at the polls. The administration is attempting to distract public attention to a purely economic question and from the colonial question. And if the people, led by this deception, return the present administration to power that act will be construed as a popular approval of the present colonialism of Porto Rico and of the future colonialism of the Philippines. If then it becomes advisable to test in the Supreme Court what the people will be alleged to have approved at the polls that also will be done. And when the Supreme Court finds that despotic government over Porto Rico is constitutional the people will in vain protest that they believed that there was no such issue as imperialism and that the currency question was paramount in 1900. The contest at that conjuncture of affairs will have been lost to the monarchial principle.

But before the people are distracted from the overshadowing issue to a mere economic problem, and before they give it into the hands of the revolutionists to say that this republican form of government has been changed by their vote, they should pause and consider the full import of the step to be taken.

The revolutionary press has already found the Porto Rican bill to be constitutional, or at least not to be incursive of anything in the constitution. The statement of the question proceeds upon a theory of interpretation entirely novel. The constitution in its entirety is not over the islands until Congress extends it to them; Congress is expressly prohibited from passing certain laws, prohibited generally and universally. These limitations are expressed in the bill of rights and in some other portions of the constitution, and, to speak specifically, as Congress is negative from passing any bill of attainder, *ex post facto* law or law prescribing any form of religion, or where Congress is otherwise limited in its power, the constitution may be said to be over the islands. In all other senses it is not over the islands. Hence, to proceed with the argument, as Congress may collect taxes, duties and imposts and as they must be "uniform throughout the United States," and as the term United States means the states and territories but not the islands, and as there is no express negation upon Congress from making duties unequal as between the United States and disconnected territory like Porto Rico, the Porto Rican bill is not unconstitutional. This is the statement that the revolutionists make of the case.

Properly, then, a brief survey of the materials which were cemented into the fabric of the republic under which we live may be indulged in to ascertain how much of truth there is in these contentions and whether it be not the fact that the republican party has perpetrated revolution and is now clamoring to obtain a vote which may be tortured into a plebiscitum[3] of revolution.

The Porto Rican law of April 12, 1900, apparently enacted at that late day so as to render its construction in the Supreme Court improbable before the election, is distinguished by the following provisions:

1. The Porto Ricans are not citizens of the United States, nor are they promised citizenship at any time whatever.

2. Porto Rico is not a territory of the United States preparing itself for statehood, but it is a colonial dependency and no statehood is promised or foreshadowed.

3. The Porto Ricans have no representation in Congress.

4. The Porto Ricans are taxed without such representation, which was formerly denounced tyranny.

5. The Porto Ricans, while declared to be citizens of Porto Rico are under the effect, the provision, and the spirit of the Porto Rican law subjects of the United States.

6. The upper house of Porto Rico is appointed by the president of the United States and is called the executive council, and this executive council has the power of passing upon the qualification of voters for the lower house.

7. No person can be a member of the lower house unless he possesses in his own right taxable property.

8. The governor is appointed by the president and has the power to veto all legislation.

9. There is a two-edged tariff of 15 per centum between the United States and Porto Rico.

10. The supreme judges of Porto Rico are appointed by the president and the local judges by the governor, an appointee of the president.

11. All the salaries of the president's appointees are to be paid by the Porto Ricans.

That our fathers should have resisted with their life's blood the assertion of wrongs like the foregoing as against them, and then that they should have formulated a constitution which by the force of its sovereignty or its implied powers or the absence in it of proper limitations permits the perpetration of the same wrongs as against other peoples is precisely what the revolutionists ask us to believe. Great Britain pursued the same policy toward the colonies of America as the present administration is pursuing toward Porto Rico under the Porto Rican law of April 12, 1900.

On May 17, 1763, the British parliament passed the "molasses act," which levied a high tax against the importation in the colonies of sugars, syrups and molasses.

On April 5, 1764, the British parliament passed the "sugar act," which levied heavy duties, not only upon sugar, but upon everything else that could be worn, eaten or used by the Americans. And the money so raised was to be paid to the crown and by the crown used to pay colonial governors and judges and twenty regiments of troops to be kept standing for their support and to overawe discontent by the arm of the military.

On March 22, 1765, the British parliament passed the stamp act, by which a heavy tax was paid upon every paper filed in court, every copy or probate of a will, every deed, bond, note, lease, conveyance or contract; every pamphlet, newspaper, advertisement, almanac, policy of insurance and other things far too numerous to mention. Certain violations of this act were punishable by death.

The American people were driven to frenzy by these despotic measures. The king answered their complaints by the "quartering act" of April, 1765, by which large bodies of troops were to be sent to America and quartered in the houses of Americans, in order to render "his majesty's" dominions more secure and to suppress anarchy and rebellion and effectually to enforce the principle that the "king hath and of right ought to have full power and authority to make laws and statues of sufficient force and validity to bind the colonies and people of America subjects of the crown of Great Britain and in all cases whatsoever."

The course of the British government tending uniformly toward more outrageous oppression, delegates from Massachusetts, Connecticut, Rhode Island, New York, New Jersey, Pennsylvania, Delaware, Maryland and South Carolina met in New York on October 7, 1765, and on the 19th of that month these delegates, calling themselves the stamp congress, adopted resolutions against the British government. Among other things they resolved:

"That it is essential to the freedom of the people and the undoubted right of Englishmen that no taxes be imposed on them but with their own consent, given personally or by their representatives. That the people of these colonies are not and from their local circumstances cannot be represented in the house of commons in Great Britain. That the only representatives of the people of these colonies are persons chosen therein by themselves and that no taxes ever have been or can be constitutionally imposed on them but by their respective legislatures."

Patrick Henry in the house of burgesses of Virginia on May 30, 1765, offered a resolution embodying the same ideas, which was adopted.[4]

On March 12, 1773, the Virginia house of burgesses thought proper to adopt some means of obtaining ready intelligence of new acts of despotism on the part of Great Britain, which were following each other with startling rapidity. Therefore Richard Henry Lee,[5] Benjamin

Harrison,[6] Thomas Jefferson, all of whom afterward signed the declaration of independence with others, were appointed a committee of correspondence.

On June 17, 1774, the house of Massachusetts, under the leadership of Samuel Adams, resolved that committees from all the colonies should be called to consider the acts of parliament. The house appointed Samuel Adams, John Adams and Robert T. Paine,[7] all of whom signed the declaration of independence, with others, as a committee to call this congress. They issued a call for delegates to meet in Philadelphia on September 5, 1774. They did meet, and the Carpenters' Association of Philadelphia, corresponding to a union of this day, tendered their hall to the delegates. Here in this humble chamber the presence of Omniscient Justice was invoked to judge of the rectitude of their intentions, and in the most noble, serious and candid mood that men ever assumed for the consideration of the gravest questions of life these delegates proceeded to pass judgment upon the acts of the crown. Who were present? George Washington, Patrick Henry, Richard Henry Lee, Samuel Adams, John Adams, John Jay, John Rutledge,[8] Peyton Randolph,[9] Roger Sherman,[10] and others. Some of these afterward signed the declaration of independence, the articles of confederation and the constitution.

On October 14, 1774, the first continental congress resolved that the American people "are entitled to life, liberty and property," and "they have never ceded to any foreign power whatever a right to dispose of either without their consent." That the crown had no right to "tax the Americans externally or internally" for raising a "revenue in America without their consent;" that "keeping a standing army in these colonies in times of peace without the consent of the legislature of that colony is against law." That legislative power invested in a "council appointed during pleasure by the crown is unconstitutional, dangerous and destructive to the freedom of American legislation."

On October 20, 1774, the American colonies entered into an association to obtain redress and to refrain from importations, and therefore the payment of the taxes imposed. And that association was provided to be maintained until the obnoxious acts of parliament were repealed.

On June 23, 1775, the continental congress appointed John Rutledge, William Livingston,[11] Benjamin Franklin, John Jay and Thomas

Johnson[12] as a committee to draw up a "declaration of the causes of taking up arms against Great Britain," to be published "by General Washington upon his arrival at the camp before Boston." Jefferson and Dickinson were added to the committee. Of these William Livingston and Franklin afterward signed the constitution; Franklin signed both the declaration of independence and the constitution and Thomas Jefferson signed the declaration of independence. In this declaration of causes it was declared that the colonies had been taxed without representation; that nothing was so dreadful as a foreign yoke and voluntary slavery; that they would not "tamely surrender that freedom which we received from our gallant ancestors," being "with one mind resolved to die freemen rather than to live slaves."

On July 4, 1776, the unanimous declaration of the thirteen United States of America was published, commonly called the declaration of independence. And this document, among other things, announced the following causes which had impelled the colonies to separate from Great Britain: "For imposing taxes upon us without our consent," "for quartering large bodies of armed troops among us," "for making judges dependent upon his (the king's) will alone for the tenure of their offices and the amount and payment of their salaries." And by way of preamble they declared, not that the Americans were born equal with the English. As Abraham Lincoln said, the declaration was not merely revolutionary. It also laid down basic truths applicable to all men and all times in all places—that "all men are created equal and endowed with the inalienable rights of life, liberty and the pursuit of happiness," just as the first continental congress resolved and in almost the same language on October 14, 1774, when Washington, Jay, John Adams, Samuel Adams and others of the most sober and temperate sense were present and gave their voice to those principles.

On November 15, 1777, the congress formulated the articles of confederation. It was signed by the delegates of the several states and congress met under it on March 2, 1781. Among other things the articles provided that "the people of each state shall have free egress and regress to and from any other state and shall enjoy therein all the privileges of trade and commerce subject to the same duties, impositions and restrictions as the inhabitants thereof respectively."

On December 20, 1783, the assembly of Virginia ceded to the United States for the benefit of the states the territory northwest of the Ohio river "upon condition that it be laid out and formed into states having the rights of sovereignty, freedom and independence of the other states." And on March 1, 1784, Thomas Jefferson and James Monroe, with others, executed the deed of Virginia, conveying that territory to the United States.

On July 13, 1787, the congress, under the articles of confederation, passed an ordinance for the government of the northwestern territory, so ceded by Virginia. It was declared therein to be the purpose of that ordinance to "extend the fundamental principles of civil and religious liberty which form the basis whereon these republics, their laws and constitutions are erected," and "to fix and establish those principles as the basis of all laws, constitutions and governments which forever hereafter shall be formed in said territory." The ordinance provided for the liberties expressed afterward in the bill of rights of the constitution. It provided that as to Indians "their lands and property shall never be taken from them without their consent;" that taxes should be uniform and should be laid by the "legislatures of the district or districts or new states as in the original states," and that the constitution and government of the states to be formed out of said territory should be republican and that slavery should never exist in said territory.

The first congress which sat under the constitution passed an act in 1789 for the enforcement of the ordinance of 1787. And sixteen of the thirty-nine framers of the constitution were members of this congress and voted for the act. Robert Sherman, Robert Morris and George Clymer, who signed the declaration of independence, were included in those sixteen members mentioned. Roger Sherman and George Washington, as before shown, participated in the association of October 20, 1774, and George Washington, as president of the United States approved this bill as to the northwestern territory enforcing the ordinance of 1787.

On September 17, 1787, the constitution of the United States was signed by the delegates in congress, and this constitution reached back to the principles enunciated by the feeble legislatures of the Massachusetts and Virginia colonies and welded them indissolubly into the organic law of a "more perfect union." Representatives and direct taxes were apportioned among the several states according to their respective numbers, which numbers should be determined, in a manner since amended, excluding, however, "Indians not taxed." Duties, imports and excises were provided to be uniform throughout the states and to be levied to pay debts and provide for the common defense and welfare. No preference was to be given over the ports of any state; no duties should be laid on the exports of any state; the citizens of each state had the rights, privileges and immunities of the citizens in the several states and were declared to be entitled to the equal protection of the laws.

The constitution was adopted to secure the blessings of that liberty which had been acquired in the revolutionary war. Of course the constitution does not expressly say that congress shall not tax people outside of the states living in a disconnected territory without giving them representation. It does not say that the people of the islands of the sea shall be forever free from the dominion of congress or the president. How could the fathers anticipate such a contingency as that? Could they foresee that the constitution would be held by this generation not to forbid that form of oppression as to islanders of the sea which the arbitrary power of parliament had imposed upon the American colonists? They did all that men could have done, by devotion, by money, by all forms of sacrifice and by their lives, to embody into the organic law of the land the great principle that taxation and representation must go hand in hand and that taxation without representation is tyranny.

Can therefore a republic so founded be constitutionally capable of tyranny? The men had gone to war because they were taxed without representation; because no tax could be imposed upon the colonists without their consent; because they were entitled to life, liberty and property, and no foreign power had the right to dispose of either without their consent. These principles characterize every document and every organic instrument executed by them and were reiterated by them on all official occasions so as never to leave any doubt that they regarded these things as axiomatic and cardinal truths, absolutely impregnable from assault or qualification.

The declaration and resolves of the first continental congress of October 14, 1774, contained the same principles as the declaration of independence expressed in practically the same language. And yet among those who were in that congress and who also signed the constitution of the United States we find the names of George Washington, John Rutledge and Roger Sherman.

Those who signed both the declaration of independence and the articles of confederation were:

Josiah Bartlett,	Thomas McKean,
Samuel Adams,	John Penn,
Elbridge Gerry,	Francis Lewis,
Roger Sherman,	John Witherspoon,
Samuel Huntington,	Richard Henry Lee,
Oliver Wolcott,	Francis Lightfoot Lee.
Robert Morris,	

Those who signed the articles of confederation and the constitution were:

Roger Sherman,	Gouverneur Morris,
Robert Morris,	Daniel Carroll.

Those who signed the declaration of independence and the constitution were:

Roger Sherman,	Robert Morris,
Benjamin Franklin,	George Clymer,
James Wilson,	George Reed.

In 1803, when Louisiana was acquired, and in 1819, when Florida was acquired, no one dreamed of perpetuating a colonial government upon either of them. Their inhabitants were made citizens. Their territory was prepared for the creation of sovereign states, as the northwestern territory had been prepared by the ordinance of 1787 and the act of congress of 1789. When the Mexican territory was acquired in 1848 the treaty provided that the Mexicans were free to retain the title and rights of Mexican citizens or to acquire those of citizens of the United States, and the executive policy of President Polk was in strict harmony with the fundamental principles which had been endowed with immortal life and vigor by Washington, Franklin, Jefferson, Jay, Sherman and the other fathers of American liberty.

When the Mexican treaty was ratified James Buchanan, secretary of state under Polk, announced the following policy as to California, which had been ceded by that treaty:

"This government de facto will, of course, exercise no power inconsistent with the provisions of the constitution of the United States, which is the supreme law of the land. For this reason no import duties can be levied in California on articles the growth, produce or manufacture of the United States, as no such duties can be imposed in any other part of our Union on the productions of California.

"Nor can new duties be charged in California upon such foreign productions as have already paid duties in any of our ports of entry, for the obvious reason that California is within the territory of the United States."

This precedent was followed when Alaska was acquired. In 1820 Chief Justice Marshall, who had been in the revolutionary war and who had a concrete knowledge that that war was waged against taxation without representation, decided that duties, imposts and excises must be uniform as between the states and the District of Columbia. And he wrote: "The District of Columbia, or the territory west of the Missouri, is not less within the United States than Maryland or Pennsylvania; and it is not less necessary that uniformity in the imposition of import duties and excises should be observed in the one than in the other."

The defenders of the present revolutionary administration argue that this decision of Marshall's is not binding because Marshall was called upon to pass on the status of the District of Columbia and not upon that of Missouri or a territory. The revolutionists further say that the Dred Scott case, which held that there is "no power given by the constitution to the federal government to establish colonies to be governed at its pleasure,"[13] was reversed by the battle of Gettysburg. But Lincoln in his oration at that battle field declared in effect that it was the declaration of independence which had there received a new baptism, which declaration of independence must be repealed in order to carry on colonialism.

But in view of the traditions of the revolutionary war, which was a concrete struggle on this self-same question of taxation, it is too obvious for discussion and admits of no denial that the McKinley administration has perpetuated revolution in the form of this government. What is there in the constitution to have prevented Porto Rico from being treated as a territory advancing to statehood, or even as to a state presently to be formed? What is there in the constitution to have prevented due observance of that principle that taxation and representation go hand in hand, and that life, liberty and the pursuit of happiness are inalienable rights?

These principles were grappled into the adamant of all American charters, including the constitution, with hooks of steel, and were welded there by the fierce heat of an eight-year struggle never to be dislodged except by a blast of revolution. But as the English were determined that the American colonists should not participate in the political power of Great Britain, but should be used for the purpose of commercial profit, so do the revolutionists now proceed upon that theory as to the Porto Ricans.

It was a significant thing that the English government annexed the Boer republics on July 4, 1900,[14] the one hundred and twenty-fourth anniversary of our declaration that taxation without representation is tyranny, and a few weeks after the McKinley administration had repudiated that doctrine by the Porto Rican bill. The English celebrated the confession of our error on the anniversary of the day when we committed it. And so the administration was estopped to decry the strangulation of the Boer republics when it had assassinated in our own midst the republican principle which caused the revolutionary war and armed the patriots to secure liberty and independence. The English had good cause for rejoicing on the anniversary of the declaration of independence in 1900.

What is the Porto Rican bill, therefore, but an act of revolution having the full effect of changing the form of government and extinguishing the soul of liberty in the constitution? The American colonists had no representation in parliament, nor have the Porto Ricans in congress, with or without the privilege of debate. The American colonists were subjects of the crown; the Porto Ricans have been made subjects of the

United States. The councils of American colonists were appointed by the crown; the executive council of Porto Rico is appointed by the president. The governors of the colonists were appointed by the crown and had the power of veto; the governor of Porto Rico is appointed by the president and has the power of veto. The crown taxed the colonists without representation; the United States by the Porto Rican bill tax the Porto Ricans without representation. The crown's appointees in the colonies were paid by the Americans; the president's appointees in Porto Rico are paid by the Porto Ricans.

How are these revolutionary policies justified? On the ground that only part of the constitution is over Porto Rico, and that as to the part that is not over Porto Rico the congress has despotic power.

The Porto Rican bill is declared by the revolutionists to be the forerunner of a like bill as to the Philippines. The Filipinos know this. They also know and believe that President McKinley was right when he said that "forcible annexation is criminal aggression," and, believing these words, they have taken encouragement from them and are resisting criminal aggression. But suppose the supreme court decides that the constitution is over the islands where the congress is expressly restrained and that it is not otherwise over the islands; that in consequence the Porto Rican act is constitutional, not because it is warranted by words in the constitution, but because it is not expressly prohibited by words in the constitution—what will be the status of the republic?

Will the people have the courage to say that such a decision cannot prescribe a rule of political action which shall be binding on future presidents and congresses? Or will they tamely submit as upon a question irrevocably and firmly settled? To this point does the Porto Rican bill conduct a republic which grew out of resistance to taxation without representation.

Notes

1. This is in reference to the administration of William McKinley. Vice President Theodore Roosevelt succeeded him as president.

2. Masters references the Organic Law Act of 1900. The act later became known as the Foraker Act after its sponsor, Joseph B. Foraker (1846–1917). The Foraker

Act effectively denied Puerto Rico the right to statehood and established an executive council to govern the colony similar to the British Crown's governing of American colonial possessions. Edgardo Meléndez, "Citizenship and the Alien Exclusion in the Insular Cases: Puerto Ricans in the Periphery of American Empire," *Centro Journal* 25, no. 1 (Spring 2013): 109–10.

3. "A law enacted by the common people, under the superintendence of the tribune or some subordinate plebian magistrate, without the intervention of the senate." *Webster's Complete Dictionary of the English Language* (London: George Bell and Sons, 1886), s.v. "plebiscitum."

4. In response to the Stamp Act, Patrick Henry (1736–99) proposed seven resolutions to the Virginia House of Burgesses in order to protect the rights of American colonists. Five of the seven resolutions were passed by the House and adopted on December 14, 1765.

5. Richard Henry Lee (1732–94) was a colonial legislator from Virginia who served in the House of Burgesses and was a fervent opponent of the Stamp Act. Lee later served on multiple Continental Congresses, where he argued for independence and for the appointment of George Washington as commander of the Continental army.

6. Benjamin Harrison (1726–91) was a member of the Virginia House of Burgesses and signer of the Declaration of Independence. Harrison was elected governor of Virginia in 1782.

7. Robert Treat Paine (1731–1814) was a lawyer and signer of the Declaration of Independence, representing Massachusetts.

8. John Rutledge (1739–1800) was a representative of South Carolina at the Stamp Act Congress. Rutledge played a key role in drafting the U.S. Constitution.

9. Peyton Randolph (1721–75) frequently led the Virginia delegation to Congress and served as the first president of the Continental Congress in 1774.

10. Roger Sherman (1721–93) was a lawyer from Connecticut who signed the Declaration of Independence, the Articles of Confederation, and the Constitution. Sherman was later elected to the first U.S. Congress in 1789.

11. William Livingston (1723–90) was a lawyer and political essayist who served on the First and Second Continental Congresses. Livingston strongly supported American independence and eventually became the first governor of New Jersey.

12. Thomas Johnson (1732–1819) was a Maryland delegate to the first Constitutional Convention. Johnson was also the first governor of Maryland and as an associate justice of the U.S. Supreme Court.

13. The original quote is, "There is certainly no power given by the Constitution to the Federal Government to establish or maintain colonies bordering on the United States or at a distance, to be ruled and governed at its own pleasure;

nor to enlarge its territorial limits in any way, except by the admission of new States." In *Dred Scott v. Sanford* (1857), Chief Justice Roger Taney argued that enslaved people maintained their enslaved status while residing in states where slavery was illegal and that, as a Black man, Scott's claim had no standing before the court. While Taney's argument here supports Masters's anti-imperialism, his use of Taney's arguments from the *Dred Scott* decision is nevertheless confusing: Taney's arguments were made in a different circumstance regarding territories contiguous to the United States, while Masters uses Taney's arguments here in regard to overseas colonies.

14. This is in reference to the Second Boer War (1899–1902), in which the British Empire fought the independence of the Boer Republics of South Africa. See Denis Judd and Keith Surridge, *The Boer War* (New York: Palgrave Macmillan, 2003).

THE PHILIPPINE
CONQUEST

D URING the campaign of 1900[1] the argument advanced against
the Philippine aggression was the repudiation of the fundamental principles of the republic involved in that aggression.
And coupled with this was the claim of injustice being perpetrated
against a helpless people. The problem now seems to be what guaran-
tees have the people at home against infractions of their liberties and
why may not the limitless power of a "sovereign" nation be directed
against them when the apparent exigency arises in favor of those who
control the government? For when a principle is once undermined the
principle can no longer be looked to for security. It is then a question
of chance as to the means of redress and protection.

Since then the constitution and the declaration have been duly rav-
ished. The country has settled down to hear the reports of pillage, murder and rapine in the islands in the great work of destroying an Asiatic
republic. Plutocracy proceeds with solemnity and dispatch to gather in
the insular concessions or to obstruct all policies when the concessions
are not readily granted. The people at large are paying the taxes and
undergoing the obvious moral decline which has set in. In short it is
discovered that the United States have embarked on a colonial policy,
but not the colonial policy of England today. It is the colonial policy of

the England of 1776, maintained to build up a nation of customers for the benefit of a favored class at home. And so we find American ideas sacrificed not merely to commercialism but to special privilege. The people furnish the soldiers; the people pay the taxes; the people build the ships, and the trusts gather in the spoils.

This revolution in our government and ideals has been accomplished by wrenching the fundamental law and the fundamental sentiments of a whole people once devoted to liberty. The whole of society has been shaken. The evil passions, the evil ambitions of men are kept down in a large measure by the unwritten law of ideals which have become intrenched by centuries of indoctrination. There is no written penalty affixed to selfishness, cruelty, lying, hypocrisy, greed, dishonor or hatred or the other demons of human nature exorcised or controlled by the power of civilization. But when the rigor of those ideals is loosened at the top the whole system of morals suffers a relaxation and a relapse. A president may initiate the catastrophe, but its impulse will recoil upon him. The congressman and the senator will feel released from the strict course of rectitude. The judge on the bench will see in the life about him and the policies about him excuse for yielding to the gathering pressure. All other officials will be similarly affected. The influence will creep into private life. It will dominate the relations between men in business and in society. All principles, whether of government or of individuals, become affected. The highwayman[2] in the alley knows what is going on and merely raves at the system that marks him out for sure punishment. At last it is only a mask that conceals the bloated face of society. There is nothing left but organized hypocrisy.

We all expect men as individuals to be more or less illogical. Life is illogical. History is illogical. Governmental policy is still more illogical. But there is a limit to its illogic. When it reaches that point morals are prostrated upon their foundations. A president may change his mind—but not from the right to the wrong. He may contradict himself—but not in the same breath. He may preach one thing and do another—but circumstances must change. There must be reason for such alterations; there must be sound sentiment for them. If these are absent it will not be long until the humblest man in the land will understand. And if the president may do such things why not himself? It is a question of example. If there ever was an irrational war it was the war with Spain. Americans deride the French as mercurial, sentimental, unsubstantial. And yet what appeared to be the American people demanded war with Spain. The Spaniards were governing without the consent of the governed, but they were willing to concede more than we have conceded. Weyler had instituted the reconcentrado camps,[3] but Spain had yielded on that point. The homes of the islanders were being burned, the people were being butchered and the horrors of war hovered over the desolate land. But they promised to end the war. Spain confessed the objections to her course. And yet there must be war. The Maine incident[4] was eliminated from the controversy by a court of our own selection. And yet there must be war. And the war came.

Then the American people beheld the United States move up and occupy the place vacated by Spain. We took their war and their methods. We tricked the Filipinos, we shot them, we burned their homes. We adopted Weyler's reconcentrado policy. We taxed them without representation. We put ourselves in the position where a combination of powers could drive us out for the same reason that we drove out Spain, and thereby make us a theme for epic laughter as long as the world should stand. Does the whole of history furnish so illogical a chapter? It seems too puerile to believe of a great nation which traces its liberties to the time when our ancestors were wild men in the north of Germany and when, as barbarians in the British Isles, they resisted Caesar and threw off the yoke of benevolent assimilation. The moral effect of such a course of shuffling and hypocrisy cannot be calculated because it is likely to affect untold generations.

At the very outset of the scheme of conquering the Filipinos it was known that the theory of the army had to be changed. Conquest cannot be left to a citizen soldiery, because volunteers fight for a principle. They fight for their rights and their homes. Such were our soldiers before imperialism became a national dream. With the volunteers we had twice driven back the hosts of monarchy. With volunteers we had met and defeated the greatest Anglo-Saxon army that ever took the field. And yet for the purpose of conquering a people armed in part with primitive weapons the creation of a regular soldiery many times its former size was demanded. This is what Gibbon[5] wrote about the two kinds of armies:

"In the purer days of the (Roman) commonwealth the use of arms was reserved for those ranks of the citizens who had a country to love, a property to defend and some share in enacting the laws, which it was their interest as well as duty to maintain. But in proportion as the public freedom was lost in extent of conquest war was gradually improved into an art and depraved into a trade."

There is no trouble about the size of the army. It is too large for legitimate purposes. But it is not large enough to be a necessary menace. The trouble is that the theory of our soldiery has been changed. Small in comparison as it is, it is the army of an empire and not of a republic. Our soldiers in the Philippines are not fighting for any principle. They are not defending their homes. They are not staying aggression. They are not repelling an attack upon liberty. There is no sentiment in the struggle. There is no conscience in the fight. It is of no consequence to our soldiers whether they win or lose, except as a matter of honor, advancement and money. For these they are there to conquer, as the Arabs were in Spain, as Spain was in Peru and Mexico, and as Great Britain is in south Africa. To conquer for spoils not for themselves, because they are only hired men, but for the trusts at home—as the Spanish regulars fought for gold for the sovereign, as the Englishman is fighting for the banks of London.

We have been assured by those who have made this army that it is too small to be dangerous to the people at home. But the real danger lies in the change of our ideals. For if a small army can be created for oppression and conquest a large army can be created for the same purpose when a large army is required. And the precedent is already established for the use of such an army at home against the sullen discontent that has already been sown among the people.

This unaccountable revolution was not accomplished without fraud and force, and that more subtle form of coercion known as freedom with starvation. Professors were driven from their chairs, the pulpit was silenced, the press gagged, officials were retired to private life and a spirit of falsehood and misrepresentation pervaded the atmosphere.

Imperialism cannot succeed without the satanic influences of life, and these came to the front with promises and threats, with dissimulation and with bribery, with every art that will persuade, silence, repress or purchase. And so as consequences of such an initiation it has followed that freedom of speech is denied; that debate is frowned down as tiresome and intolerable, and that the post-office department has become a censor of the press invested with unbridled despotism. So long as Spain and France could repress discussion by cutting out men's tongues their forms of monarchy and privilege flourished. So long as imperialism can intercept the interchange of ideas by the modem methods of ostracism and starvation and by the prevention of discussion and publicity in all the ways in which it is done imperialism may flourish. But against reason in a fair and open field it stands no chance of success.

With steam, electricity and the printing press eliminated from the world it would require no great degree of prescience to foretell the ultimate fate of the United States. For up to this time the trend of affairs with us bears such a resemblance to the march of events in the Roman republic up to the reign of Augustus Caesar that the similarities cannot be overlooked. The constitution is a plastic receptacle into which either democracy or despotism can be poured. The insular acquisitions furnished the opportunity for a gigantic stride toward despotism. These islands, according to historic precedents, according to the spirit of the constitution, which is the declaration of independence, were bound to be treated as territories advancing toward statehood. But those who had become strong through special privilege overthrew the ideals of the republic. If these islands were under the constitution then special privilege could not enjoy its spoils in the form of tariff laws, and then a more astute set of reasoners, greedy for power, saw the long-looked-for chance to greatly centralize the government, and not only the government, but the executive branch of it. The Spooner bill[6] which invested the executive with powers equal to any sovereign on earth was the proper sequence of the plan. And, moreover, it was brought about by the congress as the Roman senate surrendered its powers to Augustus. True, the congress might repeal the Spooner bill, but the executive might veto the repeal. So how is the congress to retrieve its constitutional vigor.

Heretofore the United States have been humanitarian in their spirit, but now they are governmental. Imperialism is anti-humanitarian; the conquest of people is anti-humanitarian; the taxing of people as the Filipinos are taxed is anti-humanitarian. In short, the republican party now stands for might, for power, for glory, not realizing—or if realizing not caring— that the anti-humanitarian spirit and the passion for glory and power destroyed the governments of the past and is hastening the destruction of those of the present. That at the bottom was the real trouble, and that is the virus that has found lodgment among us. For while life is essentially selfish as a condition of self-preservation it consists with the passion for justice which both men and nations must observe or suffer the sure penalty. At last it will fully leak out and be understood by all men that the supreme court upheld the new policy on apparent grounds of expediency. It will be generally understood that the influences which had set in and which had affected every department of the government were too powerful for so worldly a tribunal to resist. For that court said in about so many words that the Porto Rican tax[7] must be constitutional, because otherwise the United States could not safely retain the islands, and, besides, any other construction might obstruct future acquisitions. The supreme court asks how can the Porto Rican tax be unconstitutional, since to hold it so would be to deprive the government of that discretionary power absolutely necessary to profitably hold to the islands. The spirit of this reasoning will eventually produce wide national consequences.

All things having worked out so well to this pass, the accession of Mr. Roosevelt to the presidency was dramatically fitting. If made to order it could not have been better. He will pass into history as the contemporary of Kipling[8] and William of Germany.[9] He is of them and of their spirit and day. Some hoped that Mr. Roosevelt would throw his power on the side of idealism and progress. But they should have remembered that he repudiated his literary productions in the campaign of 1900. All his fine pretensions went the way of the world; nor in any event is he the man to stand out against the accumulated influences of imperialism. He has and will add to them. For, unspeakable as was the assassination of Mr. McKinley,[10] it was not political, and it cannot in candor be made the popular opportunity for suppressing the freedom of speech. It is very significant also that Mr. Roosevelt should inform us that such tragic episodes will merely result in the accession of men to the presidency who are merciless and resolute. How is such a deplorable change to come about? How shall we descend from a Washington to an Alexander of Farnese?[11] And why should he tell us that the one lurid moment of anarchistic triumph would be followed by centuries of despotism? Is the republic on so rocking a foundation as this?

And how is that despotism to come about? Will he be a party to it, or will he in any supreme moment of moral trial return to the apothegms of his books and say, as he has often said, "We have work to do and the only question is whether we will do it well or ill?" It is now his time to invoke the humanitarian spirit and turn from power and glory if he would give the world the moral impulse that men of his own race gave to the world centuries ago. Otherwise, if centralization in government continues and the people are more generally deprived of the chance to obey the better instructions of their natures what may be expected? Not merely a return to the method of selecting presidential electors by the legislatures, as was formerly done, and the rise of a man merciless and resolute to the presidency. A greater reaction than this may be expected.

There is a commonplace optimism which insists that either everything is for the best or that the right is predestined to triumph. Both propositions are false. Very many things are for the worse. Whole nations have gone down to destruction as the result of the excesses, the follies and the villainies of aristocracies.

That nothing can be hoped for from the present administration; that its ideals are wholly wrong; that its desires are selfish, reactionary and despotic, and that it is capable of any perfidy, is a pardonable pessimism. The optimism to be cherished consists in the belief that democracy is not the battle cry of a fraction of men, but that it is a passion, a philosophy, an ineradicable aspiration of the human heart. Armies and navies may be created and the people may be taxed to support them; expensive flummery and glitter may be maintained out of the sweat of labor. All of this may be used to trample down justice and to despoil a helpless race. And yet in the heart of the humblest man there remains the belief that he has a right in this world to live, to labor, to earn and be free. The most ignorant tribes of the Filipinos are equal in intelligence to the natives of Britain in the days of the glorious Julius. Who knows what use the Filipinos may make of our ideals and the spirit of freedom which vibrates in their hearts today? And who knows what will be the relative positions of the Philippine islands and what we now call the United States 1,000 years hence? The thought should teach humility. For did Augustus imagine that the unconquerable Belgae[12] would found a great republic, or that the savages in the worthless islands north of Gaul would produce those great luminaries of civilization before whom Cicero[13] and Virgil[14] pale their ineffectual fires?

Notes

1. In this presidential campaign, Democratic candidate William Jennings Bryan (1860–1925) ran against Republican candidate William McKinley; McKinley was the victor in the 1900 election.

2. Another name for a robber.

3. General Valeriano Weyler (1838–1930) was named governor of Cuba in 1896. With full powers granted to him, Weyler set up *reconcentrado* camps to hold Cuban civilians and protect them with Cuban freedom fighters until after the war. However, the camps were poorly maintained and proved inhumane to the Cuban occupants. David Silbey, *A War of Frontier and Empire: The Philippine-American War, 1899–1902* (New York: Hill and Wang, 2007), 11, 32–33.

4. On February 15, 1898, The USS *Maine* inexplicably exploded in the Havana, Cuba, harbor, causing the United States to blockade Cuba and wage war against Spain. Louis A. Pérez Jr., "The Meaning of the *Maine*: Causation and the Historiography of the Spanish-American War," *Pacific Historical Review* 58, no. 3 (1989): 293–322.

5. Edward Gibbon (1737–94). Gibbon was an English historian known for writing *The History of the Decline and Fall of the Roman Empire* (1776). See James Westfall Thompson, "Edward Gibbon, 1737–1794," *Pacific Historical Review* 7, no. 2 (1938): 93–119.

6. The Spooner bill or Spooner Amendment (1901) gave the U.S. government the authority to "maintain a temporary civil government" for as long as it felt necessary over the Philippine Islands during the Philippine-American War. See J. A. Robertson, "The Effect in the Philippines of the Senate 'Organic Act,'" *Journal of Race and Development* 6, no. 4 (1916): 370–87.

7. The Puerto Rican tax reassessed land taxes in Puerto Rico; the new tax law was based on the quality and type of usage of the land. It benefited U.S. sugar corporations while putting a heavy tax burden on non-landowners in Puerto

Rico. See Diane Lourdes Dick, "U.S. Tax Imperialism in Puerto Rico," *American University Law Review* 65, no. 1 (2015): 1–86.

8. Rudyard Kipling was an English author who penned a highly influential poem titled "The White Man's Burden," the work most likely being referenced here, which was originally published in the *London Times* (1899).

9. Wilhelm II of Germany, the last German emperor, who came to be known for his attempts at a "personal" or absolutist rule, "his desire for public celebration and recognition . . . sometimes ridiculous self-display," and unstable foreign affairs. These elements of his political policy are believed to be underlying causes of the outbreak of World War I. See Annika Mombauer and Wilhelm Deist, eds., *The Kaiser: New Research on Wilhelm II's Role in Imperial Germany* (Cambridge: Cambridge University Press, 2003), 2.

10. On September 6, 1901, an anarchist named Leon Czolgosz (1873–1901) shot president William McKinley, who was visiting the Pan-American Exposition in New York; he died on September 14. Czolgosz felt that McKinley represented oppression and believed it was his duty to eliminate him.

11. Alexander Farnese (1545–92) was the Duke of Parma in Italy in the sixteenth century known for his skills as a soldier. See M. R. Madden, "Alexandre Farnèse, Prince de Parme, Gouverneur Général des Pays-Bas (1545-1592) by Léon van der Essen," *Catholic Historical Review* 21, no. 2 (1935): 203–8.

12. The Belgae were a confederation of Celts living in what is now France during the first century. Michael M. Sage, *The Republican Roman Army: A Sourcebook* (New York: Routledge, 2008), 134.

13. Marcus Tullius Cicero (106–43 BCE) was a Roman political and philosophical writer. After denouncing Mark Antony, Cicero was executed. See Richard Leo Enos and Dean N. Constant, "A Bibliography of Ciceronian Rhetoric," *Rhetoric Society Quarterly* 6, no. 2 (1976): 21–28.

14. Publius Vergilius Maro (70–19 BCE) was a Roman poet best known for his work *The Aeneid,* which is a Roman interpretation of Homer's *The Odyssey.* See Shirley Werner, "Vergilian Bibliography 2019–2020," *Vergilius* 66 (2020): 163–85.

THE NEW POLICY

SINCE the campaign of 1900 a good deal has been spoken and written concerning the plight of the democratic party. That of itself can be of little consequence except as that plight affects those principles upon which the welfare of the whole people depends. But in so far as democratic defeat has introduced mischievous and perilous conditions into American polity, the plight of that party must come home to all Americans with a message of grave significance.

The republic was born of political idealism. If it had sprung from expediency—that is, from a desire to put away present evil—nothing more would have been necessary than a declaration of war against Great Britain. Such a declaration could have been made good by force of arms. And a government of some form could have been founded growing out of the mere selfish, but proper, impulse on the part of our forefathers to have a government of their own. But our forefathers went much farther than that. They spoke not only for themselves, but for all people and for all time. They laid down political principles in precise and comprehensive language. Were those principles true? The English derided them, although we are told that "there are certain principles of natural justice inherent in the Anglo-Saxon character which need no expression in constitutions." The English found a violent conflict between the utterances of the declaration of independence and those "principles of justice inherent in the Anglo-Saxon character."[1] It resulted that the declaration triumphed through war over those Anglo-Saxon principles and the republic was born.

But after these things had happened did the fathers go about to construct a government which could perpetrate against some other people the oppressions which the English had perpetrated upon them? Was it only their taxation without representation which constituted tyranny? And did they immediately put into action a government which could, according to expediency, tax some other people without representation? It is to this pass of vulgarity and cynicism that the argument is reduced which seeks to extract from the silence of the constitution a power in congress to tax the Porto [sic] Ricans without representation.

The words liberty and freedom are words of general significance and mean everything or nothing, according to the peculiar views of him who uses them. They are found in magna charta. But magna charta did not prevent James II from overriding the most sacred rights of liberty. This infamous despot habitually assured the English people that he stood for liberty even while a slavish parliament cooperated with him in the destruction of human rights and human life. This was only a little over 200 years ago and "the principles of natural justice inherent in the Anglo-Saxon character" laid no obstacles in the way of the bloody assize and the temporary extinguishment of every ray of liberty. Except for the infusion of republicanism which came with William from Holland[2] the English would have had no more to boast of in the way of inherent principles than the Russians. And the English constitution would have been even more vague and elastic than it is.

When our fathers adopted the constitution the English parliament, in the language of Mr. Bryce, had the same powers which it has today, as follows: "It can make and unmake any and every law, change the form of the government or the succession to the crown, interfere with the course of justice, extinguish the most sacred private rights of the citizen. Between it and the people at large there is no legal distinction. It is, therefore, within its sphere of law irresponsible and omnipotent."[3]

Did the fathers then intend to make congress an "irresponsible and omnipotent" body upon the theory that those "principles of natural justice" would be sufficient limitation upon congressional despotism?

That is the argument, and that is the theory upon which the Porto Rican tariff was sustained by the supreme court.

The opinion of the court delivered by Mr. Justice Brown is historically, legally, politically and ethically false. It is a tissue of sophistry. It is a jumble of assumption. It is a flat reversal of all former decisions. It overrides the solemn deliberations of the fathers. It incurs the sound reasonings of Jefferson, Madison, Marshall, Webster, Story, Lincoln and Taney.[4] It flies in the face of common sense. It twistifies [sic] and splits the English language into meaningless refinements in an endeavor to overcome palpable and indubitable truths written in language which does not admit of doubt. Its basic assumption is that the United States can do anything that any other nation can do. Syllogistically expressed Russia, Germany or England as sovereign powers can grab islands, rule subjects and exploit them. The United States are sovereign, and, therefore, they can do whatever Russia, Germany or England can do. It is obvious at a glance that the minor premise is false, and not only has never before been pronounced by the supreme court, but is far beyond the wildest declarations of the maddest Hamiltonian up to this day. Even Marshall when validating the United States bank did it in the name of the constitution and under an assumed power of the constitution; while the Porto Rican tariff is validated in spite of the constitution. In the bank case Marshall said: "Let the end be legitimate, let it be within the scope of the constitution, and all means which are appropriate which are plainly adapted to that end, which are not prohibited, but consist with the letter and spirit of the constitution are constitutional."[5] Mr. Justice Brown says the United States are as sovereign as any nation and "we decline to hold that there is anything in the constitution to prevent such action" namely, taxation without representation.

In the first place the United States have sovereign powers only within their sphere of constitutional grant, and, second, the question cannot be disposed of by the statement that there is nothing in the constitution to prevent such action. Is there anything in the constitution to permit such action, either in letter or spirit? That is the question which we have been taught by this court and constitutional writers to apply to any course of congressional or executive polity.

Said Marshall: "The government of the United States is emphatically and truly a government of the people. In fact and substance it emanates from them; its powers are granted by them and for their benefit. This government is acknowledged by all to be one of enumerated powers. The principle that it can only exercise the powers granted to it would seem too apparent to have required to be urged by all these arguments, which its enlightened friends, while it was pending before the people, found it necessary to urge. "Again Marshall said: "The government of the United States can claim no powers which are not granted to it by the constitution, and the powers actually granted must be such as are expressly given, or given by necessary implication."

Mr. Story:[6] "The constitution was from its very origin contemplated to be the frame of a national government of special and enumerated powers and not of general and unlimited powers."

Mr. Webster[7] in 1848. "Arbitrary governments may have territories and distant possessions, because arbitrary government may rule them by different laws and different systems. We cannot do such things. They must be of us, part of us, or else strangers."

William H. Seward[8]—"The framers of the constitution never contemplated colonies or provinces or territories. They contemplated nothing but sovereign states."

Mr. Cooley[9]—"The government of the United States is one of enumerated powers, the national constitution being the instrument which specifies them and in which authority should be found for the exercise of any power which the national government assumes to possess. In this respect it differs from the constitutions of the several states, which are not grants of power to the state, but which apportion and impose restrictions upon the powers which the states inherently possess."

The republican party in 1860[10]—"That we recognize the great principles laid down in the immortal declaration of independence as the true foundation of democratic government, and we hail with gladness every effort toward making these principles a living reality on every inch of American soil."

The supreme court in 1897[11]—"Absolute arbitrary power exists nowhere in this free land. The authority of the United States must be found in the constitution."

The constitution itself—"The powers not delegated to the United States by the constitution nor prohibited by it to the states are reserved to the states respectively or the people."

But there is an embarrassment of riches. Up to the Downes decision the constitutional test of a law was found in the words of Marshall already quoted. The end must be legitimate; it must be within the scope of the constitution; the means must be plainly adapted to the end; the means must not be prohibited by the constitution, but must consist with the letter and spirit of the constitution, while under the Downes decision any law which any sovereign power can enact and which is not prohibited by the constitution is constitutional. Here is a formula of revolution as complete as the most rabid monocrat could desire.

The old strict constructionists were accused of holding that the congress could pass no law unless the constitution expressly authorized it. The principle of the Downes case is strict construction on the reverse side. It declares that congress can pass any law which the constitution does not expressly inhibit. It follows that the only limitations upon congress are expressed in the bill of rights and in a few other negative clauses. Otherwise it is as powerful as the British parliament, which is also in theory restrained by a bill of rights. And, this being true, this congress can mount upon the ruins of a constitutional republic and unfurl the banner of empire. Its power does not consist within grants and prohibitions, nor yet within the implied powers of Marshallism. It has marched up to that domain where it is not expressly prohibited from going and has claimed every power not expressly denied to it.

In a sort of way the American people elect their senators; in truth and in fact they elect their representatives. They are sent to Washington, where, before entering upon their duties, they take an oath to support the constitution. If our senators and congressman have power to pass such laws—as the supreme court says they have—as the Porto Rican bill, where did they get it? It is not claimed that they got it from the constitution. They cannot get it from the states, because the supreme court expressly says that the states never at any time had power to acquire territory. They did not get it from the people because that could not be done only through a constitutional amendment. The question, then, remains, Where did they get it? Under the Porto Rican bill, so validated by the supreme court, we have left a constitution which is effective so far as it expressly restrains congress, and for the rest we have "principles of natural justice inherent in the Anglo-Saxon character." Meantime, Mr. McKinley tours the country and in effect assures the American people that their rights will remain as formerly. There will be no change at home. We have bartered a written constitution for inherent Anglo-Saxon principles and executive reassurances.

Conceding the narrow contention that the congress is not prohibited from taxing the inhabitants of an appurtenant territory according to the uniformity clause of the constitution, must not a law, according to Marshall, consist with the letter and spirit of the constitution? If the United States were a despotism or a monarchy the argument would be sound. To interpret a law of a despotic government in favor of despotism is perfectly consistent. But it is another thing to interpret the constitution of a republic in favor of despotism. It must be interpreted in favor of republicanism to be consistent. Therefore, the question is not in its nature purely constitutional. It is also fundamental. A republic by its inherent nature possesses certain characteristics. It has a spirit, which is liberty. Its very being consists in a rule of the people. A republic that stands for liberty at home and tyranny abroad as to people who cannot defend themselves has to that extent ceased to be a republic. Its own people may well be alarmed for their own liberties which are begun to be pledged to them in executive assurance and "principles of justice inherent in the Anglo-Saxon character" decreed by the supreme court.

But how soon have come true all the prophecies of democracy touching this miserable complication! Democracy attacked the validity of the treaty of Paris[12] on the plain ground that the acquisition of distant islands peopled by alien races was not an exercise of constitutional power and was repugnant to the spirit of a republic. Mr. Story had so declared in his great work on the constitution. Montesquieu had considered that question in detail. And now one of the reasons for not sustaining the ex proprio vigore[13] doctrine concerning the constitution is stated by Mr. Justice Brown to be that the executive and the senate should not be given the power to incorporate alien races into the American system by the mere fiat of a treaty. Mr. Story wrote: "If congress have the power it may unite any foreign territory whatever to our own, however distant, however populous and however powerful. Under the form of cession we may become united to a more powerful neighbor or rival and be involved in European or other foreign interests."[14] But all authority, all reason were brushed aside. And not only is the treaty to stand, ratified by the whole congress, so far as the lower branch can ratify it, but legislation is to stand of a character which provoked the American colonies to war in 1776. And because the constitution is silent on the question the highhanded and revolutionary proceeding is to be validated which, according to all authority, tends to overthrow and not to perpetuate the republic. That a congress can legislate so as to overthrow the republic is somewhat repugnant to the great argument of Mr. Webster. Democracy contended that these people could not be citizens without imperiling our own civilization. And the supreme court says that is true. Democracy said that they could not be subjects without undermining the republic; nor without depositing in its body the germ of constitutional destruction. And the supreme court offers the people "principles of justice inherent in the Anglo-Saxon character." The administration, backed by the supreme court, assures the American people that these races shall have all the liberty they are capable of enjoying. Democracy contended that even with steam and electricity the control of these distant islands would aggrandize the power of the executive, and the Spooner bill demonstrated the truth of that contention. So that every objection, though loudly derided at the time, became verified in a few months.

Even Mr. Roosevelt as a constitutional historian had declared that a republic could acquire nothing but contiguous territory capable of being formed into states; and that such territory must be peopled not at all, or by the white race fit to be incorporated into the American system. But he toured the country declaring in effect that he himself was antedated. All events have shown that he was correct when he was not seeking office. Democracy contended from the first that the whole scheme was a renaissance of mercantile colonialism; and the Porto Rican bill proved it. And thus it was demonstrated that the American republic in an hour of test did not have the moral reserve to stand by its principles. It went to war to free an oppressed people and then turned oppressor and sunk to the level of other sovereign powers in a vulgar and wholly mistaken scheme of acquiring national wealth.

And now in what plight are the American people? They had nothing to do with the treaty. It was formulated secretly by commissioners in Paris; it was consented to by a body that they do not elect. The Porto Rican bill was enacted under the party lash. It was validated by a court that is as independent of their choice as an hereditary monarch. The question of the acquisition or retention of the islands has never been passed upon at the polls, and after the election the Spooner bill created executive imperialism. The supreme court has created congressional imperialism. What are you going to do about it? What are you going to do about these events that follow so swiftly one after another and that will continue to occur? When will the supreme court catch up with the administration even if it was opposed to imperialism? What has become of your republic in four years? The fact is the republican party never since the days of Lincoln has had any principle whatever on any subject. It never had any theory of government except what it borrowed from Jefferson. It rode into power on the declaration of independence and when it abandoned the declaration through the ascendancy of rapacious federalism it went plumb into monarchy and has ever since hidden its designs from the people under the garb of holiness and patriotism. It temporized with the tariff question and met it on terms of expediency; it practiced expediency with the money question, and at all times it has followed the trail of toryism and monarchy.[15] It has built up its leaders through special privilege and it has debauched its followers with the argument that the government exists to support the people. It has awakened anarchy and touched into life that very socialism which it pretends to abhor.

And so what does the paramount party care about such rights as freedom of speech and of the press so long as it can wring tribute from dependent people? They may rail and write as they please against this great vulgar government. They may have the habeas corpus, too. Individual judges in the far islands acting under central orders will whittle away that and every other right in individual cases as circumstances require; and they will do it under that unknown clause of the constitution which makes the United States as sovereign as any other nation. A party that taxes without representation will also deprive of life and property without due process of law. The negative prohibitions of the constitution are not so much as pack thread about the arms of a republican congress.

The plight of the American people consists in this, that no peculation of any official, no disregard of plain duty, no breach of expressed faith with Cuba, no act of despotism toward our insular possessions, no disregard of the constitution, finds any response of rebuke in the breast of the republican party. It is so sunk in the depths of infamy that no imagined revolution, with all the accompaniments of monarchy, would arouse that party to protest. Things never feared but spoken of by the fathers as impossible to our system have come to pass. Colonialism is validated on the expressed ground of expediency and there is rejoicing. Retrogression is hailed as progress. All the vilest elements of human nature are sent whirling to the top of national life—cupidity, hypocrisy, dishonesty, tyranny and debauchery; we behold the destruction of ideals, the withering of character and morality and there is no protest, but rejoicing. The hideous specter of slavocracy has been tempted from the tomb to revisit the glimpses of this era and a portion of the work that this very republican party came into being to perform is being swept away amid shouts of the administration.

That corporations are corrupt, that they debauch every branch of the government has passed into the domain of jest and is tossed about in a spirit of humorous comment. Our officials are openly accused of dishonesty and corruption by the leading journals and it is accepted at large as a commonplace. The people are suspicious of their legislators and their courts. Everyone knows that the Filipinos were our allies and that we betrayed them; that we broke our word with Cuba and that the course of the president has been uncandid and inconsistent. One of the great papers declared that the decision of the supreme court was smeared with tobacco and sugar. And against this resistless tide of evil who will remain true to the ideals of morality except the strongest swimmers? Moreover, amidst all this there is a lamentable lack of good sense. Prosperity is measured by the ability of the seller to advance the price and not by the ability of the purchaser to buy. It is measured by the activity of monopolists, not by the normal activity of the people at large. It is measured by the extent to which capital consents to the employment of labor, not by the demand which the consumer calls upon the producer to produce.

But to hold society together there must be some enforcement of law. So that pinochle and larceny will be vigorously punished, while gambling in grain, monopolistic extortion, slaughter of inferior peoples and other things which extend civilization will proceed without interruption.

And what is the conclusion that is forced upon men? These degeneracies have been treated with ideals and the disease has steadily grown worse. Was not slavery destroyed by ideals? History answers this question in the negative and by so answering it declares that civilization has not yet reached the point where ideals are sufficient to work reforms. Slavery was destroyed by the power of money. Slavery was uneconomic. It crushed the south; it interfered with the rights of white labor. Yet at this the time of its overthrow, economically speaking, had not come in Lincoln's day. For slavery was still profitable to the mercantilists in the north and in England. Lincoln would not have been elected except for a split in the democratic party. In fact, he received the smallest per centum of the vote of any candidate ever elected by the American people. Colonialism does not pay; it never paid any country. It is profitable only to the privileged few. But colonialism cannot be destroyed until the forces of plutocracy become divided or until its uneconomic features bear hard enough upon a sufficient number of people to win them back to the ways of a plain but virtuous republic. Ideals will not do. We have seen that ideals are as flax to the fire in a day when men are hungry for money.

Notes

1. In *Downes v. Bidwell*, U.S. Supreme Court justice Henry B. Brown (1838–1913) justified American imperialism in these terms.

2. William III of Holland became the king of England (1689–1702); under his reign, British Parliament passed the Act of Toleration (1689), which granted freedom of religion.

3. James Bryce (1838–1922) was a British historian who wrote extensively about American political institutions. See James Bryce, *The American Commonwealth*, vol. 1, 3 vols. (London: Macmillan, 1888), 42–44.

4. Roger B. Taney, chief justice during the *Dred Scott* case, is in strange company here, since many of these figures, including Marshall and Lincoln, were advocates for robust federal powers, a notion anathema to Masters.

5. Marshall defined implied powers in *McCulloch v. Maryland*.

6. Joseph Story, Supreme Court justice (1812–45).

7. Daniel Webster, secretary of state (1841–43, 1850–52), representative (1823–27), and senator from Massachusetts (1827–41, 1845–50).

8. William Seward (1801–72), governor of New York (1839–42), senator from New York (1849–61), secretary of state (1861–69).

9. Thomas McIntyre Cooley (1824–98), chief justice of the Michigan Supreme Court (1864–85).

10. This appears in the Republican Party platform of 1868.

11. John Marshall Harlan (1833–1911), dissenting opinion, *Robertson et al. v. Baldwin* (1897).

12. In 1898, the Treaty of Paris ended hostilities between Spain and the United States, leading to Cuba's ostensible independence, the cession of Puerto Rico and Guam, and the purchase of the Philippines for $20 million. David J. Silbey, *A War of Frontier and Empire: The Philippine-American War, 1899–1902* (New York: Hill and Wang, 2007), 57–59.

13. Meaning "by its own force." John Bouvier, *A Law Dictionary, Adapted to the Constitution and Laws* . . . (Philadelphia: J. B. Lippincott, 1883), 1:618.

14. Joseph Story argued that under its implied powers, the United States could procure additional territories for inclusion in the Union. Joseph Story, *Commentaries of the Constitution of the United States; with a Preliminary Review of the Constitutional History of the Colonies and States, before the Adoption of the Constitution* (Boston: Hillard, Gray, 1833), 2:156–61.

15. The Tories were a British political party often associated with support of the monarchy, as well as hierarchy, natural order, and aristocracy.

Political Tendencies

W EBSTER, in his great political speech delivered in New York March 15, 1837,[1] used the following language in commenting upon what is now termed the "constitutional march": "A gentleman," said he, "not now living, wished very much to vote for the establishment of a bank of the United States, but he always stoutly denied the constitutional power of the United States to create such a bank. The country, however, was in a state of great financial distress, from which such an institution, it was hoped, might help to extricate it, and this consideration led the worthy member to review his opinions with care and deliberation. He came satisfactorily to the conclusion that congress might incorporate a bank. The power, he said, to create a bank was either given to congress or it was not given. Very well. If it was given congress, of course, could exercise it; if it was not given the people still retained it, and in that case congress, as the representative of the people, might upon an emergency make free use of it." Continuing the bitter irony, Webster said: "Arguments and conclusions in substance like these, gentlemen, will not be wanting if men of great popularity, commanding characters, sustained by powerful parties and full of good intentions toward the public, may be permitted to call themselves universal representatives of the people."

It is the argument that a given thing must be done and, therefore, that there must be constitutional power to do it that has led to nearly all the trespasses upon the organic law. For instance, listen to the reasoning in the decision in the insular cases:[2] "A false step at this time," said Mr. Justice Brown, "might be fatal to the development of what Chief Justice Marshall called the American empire. Choice in some cases, the natural gravitation of small bodies toward large ones in others, the result of a successful war in still others may bring about conditions which would render the annexation of distant possessions desirable."

How far annexation in any case is desirable is a difficult matter to determine. Can it be gathered from the inspired utterances of newspapers or the paid articles in magazines? Can it be gathered from the interviews of congressmen and senators or the prepared speeches of politicians engaged in creating a sentiment of desire for annexation? Can the desire of the people be ascertained unless they express themselves in a manner which separates their consideration of annexation from their consideration of all other questions? If, in fact, a majority of the people desire annexation, and if it be not merely desired by a clique of selfish commercialists, is the desire of a thing the test of constitutionality? We can paraphrase Webster's words as follows: "The power to annex islands and govern them arbitrarily outside of the constitution was either given to congress or it was not given. Very well. If it was given congress, of course, could exercise it. If it was not given the people still retain it, and in that case congress, as the representative of the people, might upon an emergency make free use of it, especially where it is desirable and where a false step at this time might be fatal to acquisitions hereafter."

"There shall be no imperialism," said the late Mr. McKinley, "except the imperialism of the American people," which means also that whatever the people desire the congress will do, congress or a few privileged interests being the judge, however, of what the people desire.

From the mocking satire of Webster to the solemn decision of Mr. Justice Brown is a long step, and yet this is one of the developments which some men yet living have seen come to pass.

The arguments which were used to create a desire for imperialism, if there was any real desire for it, and which were largely accepted, plainly show that the present sociological state of the American people is religious if not supernatural. Many well-meaning people can be won to anything by the argument that it is predestined or that it bears the evidence of a providential dispensation wonderful and particular. This appeals to the imagination and stirs the dramatic sense more or less active in all men. And though we no longer beat tomtoms to drive away eclipses nor attribute pestilence to the wrath of demons and in general have installed law and order where caprice and accident formerly held sway, yet nevertheless when a certain class of thinkers deals with the actions of large bodies of men, whether as nations or armies, their imaginations carry them completely away. If Admiral Dewey steers into the harbor of Manila without accident and defeats the Spaniards it is providential.

The Boers and the Britons prayed to the same God, yet the victory was providential and predestined.[3] A few diplomats struck with the commercial advantages of the Philippine islands negotiate for their cession in the same deliberate way that an individual buys out a business, and the cry is set up that they came to our hands by the act of God. "Whether we are glad or sorry," says Mr. Roosevelt, "that events have forced us to go there is aside from the question. The point is that as the inevitable result of the war with Spain we find ourselves in the Philippines."

It is the invention of such fictions as these and their explanation upon a supernatural basis that enables a few men to use a large contingent of well-meaning people—people who are carried away by gusts of false sentiment which they imagine to be pentecostal visitations of the oversoul.[4] Is it any wonder that the diplomats and empire builders laugh in their sleeves at the people?

But as it was our destiny to make this "desirable" annexation it is also our destiny to play a mighty part hereafter in the history of the world. There shall not be any longer a cowardly shrinking from duty; for woe or weal the die is cast. It is fate. We must fail greatly or triumph greatly, but great we must be. The past is dead; our little part of isolation is over. We are no longer the Maud Muller of nations drinking at the well, ashamed of our calico gowns and sighing for the city far away.[5] We have become great. We have painted our eyebrows and put on our scarlet robes, and, being no longer a reproach or a menace to any other power, we suddenly find ourselves on terms of kindness with all nations, except in so far as jealousy might be enkindled if expected favors should not be distributed with a decent regard to circumstances.

Yet all this talk about this nation having suddenly become an influence in the world is merely a piping upon penny whistles. For that matter the United States were a world power in 1776. The American revolution established the French republic and shook every throne in Europe. The struggle of our people in the war for independence resulted in greater rights to every man in Europe, and the end is not yet. The United States were pretty much of a world power in 1812; in the sense, moreover, in which the gentlemen use the term. They were a world power in the days of President Monroe, when we, as a little people, declared to the whole of Europe that the extension of monarchy on the western hemisphere would not be tolerated. We were something of a world power in 1861 in spite of the hatred of England, whose sudden friendship in this day makes some of us wonder. We were something of a world power in 1867 when Napoleon III was forced by President Johnson to take his troops from Mexico and leave the paper empire of Maximilian to its fate. And we were something of a world power during the administration of President Cleveland when England was frightened from Venezuela. No loving kindness at that time prevented us from protecting our interests and traditions as it does in these days of our boasted prowess as a world power.

But how long will our ideas last or the expression of them remain untrammeled? Trooping behind our entrance as a world power comes the hint that the Philippine aggression cannot be discussed without committing an impropriety. "If we are sensitive to our honor at home," says Mr. Roosevelt, "we will not discuss it." For it is a question neither of right nor wrong, nor of constitutional law, but it is a question of honor. It is fate, but if it were not fate it is done, and since done honor forbids its condemnation. Thus the constitution is made a huge joke; a genial myth like Santa Claus with which to befool the people, while everything is resolved into a question of honor, and whether our honor is being besmirched or not depends upon those to decide who assume to conserve it and fix the political fashions of the day.

Some other conditions have arisen as the outgrowth of other developments which have fully made their appearance at this time. The tendency of the period is very strongly toward socialism. That it should be condemned as unholy by the very men who have produced it is perhaps as strange a feature as the movement exhibits.

For almost a century it has been the policy to give governmental aid to men no more entitled to it than anyone else. Manufacturers have been awarded premiums of all sorts upon the theory that they were predestined to have it and inherently and of right must have it. For, it is said, they cannot be profitable without it. "The tariff," according to Mr. Roosevelt in his late message, "makes manufacturers profitable, and the tariff remedy proposed (for the trusts) would be in effect simply to make manufacturers unprofitable."

So this governmental favoritism leads not to a revival of individualism but to socialism, for the reason that long confusion of the province of the state has obscured the line between state duty and individual right and has made men eager for immediate benefits as the favorites of government have been eager for bounties and gifts in order to obtain present results. And if this dispensation of special privileges is necessary as a foundation of our modern commercialism why, it is asked, is it not the prior step in the order of evolution, or collective ownership? Hereby we eliminate the tyrannous greed of the few who use our property for our own undoing; who not only take the bulk of what we earn, but tax us for those things which we need, and which we have made it profitable to produce by tariff laws bearing upon us. Hence it is that all socialists, and especially the Marxians, watch with calm certainty the results. Their belief that by some blind fatality society is moving toward socialism and that the aggression of capital enters into the certain force which will bring the wished-for end is in part justified.

The efforts of the magicians of plutocracy to keep back the ground swell are wasted in air. Not realizing that their patrons have produced the movement, they seem to think that it can be kept down by shouting socialism or by talking against "criminal discontent," "vile trade unions" and other disorders. One distinguished educator grieves because it seems to him that labor wishes to "work as few hours as possible and get as much money as possible"—just as if it had been the creed of capitalism to give as much as possible and exact as little as possible.

What a spectacle has been held up to the wealth producers of this country for more than a century! They have seen every form of capitalism lobbying at the national and state capitals for laws enabling them to get something for nothing. They have seen the laws made and administered for their interests. They have seen protected industries combine with each other to monopolize and extort, and railroads combine with these to discriminate against and crush out independent enterprise. They have seen some of their sworn officials uphold this condition as scientific, the result of natural evolution, and others confess its iniquities, but deny their power under the constitution to help it. Why should moral wonders be expected of labor? Too great a compliment is paid it in marveling that it desires short hours and big pay. It sees corruption and favoritism flourish at the top and the laws of supply and demand and competition repealed from the industrial code, and in consequence it can conceive no reason why it should not become an actor in the great melodrama of "grab."

But if socialism shall come, what then? Democracy has not failed because it has not been tried. Our ills have followed from violations of democracy and not because of its observance. It is trite enough to say, but not sufficiently learned, nevertheless, that this government was founded upon the principle of equal rights. If that had been observed it seems inconceivable that we should suffer from the present evils. If it could be proven that the great industries of the land and our great industrial system could not have been built up except by special privilege yet has the end justified the means? Build up a few, but impoverish the many. The country as a whole is no richer. It is an argument that ends where it begins, except that human blood is consumed in its development. And that is the question. Are men but coral insects that build and die? Are we on a level with animals which devour each other for sustenance? This is where the argument ends; only the preachers and the teachers indulge in irrelevant conclusions of some sort; or latterly they have canonized Darwin and driven self-conscious intelligence in the control of human destiny from the economic field.

Lastly collectivism is the opposite of individualism. Perhaps a partial trial of the former might prove its own undoing and carry with it the downfall of paternalism as well. The pendulum ought to swing that way. If it did the cost would not be too much for the benefit derived.

Notes

1. Senator Daniel Webster delivered this speech at Niblo's Saloon in New York to a crowd of citizens and an assembled committee that sought to welcome and commend Webster. His speech was given in response to their observations on his "great talents, great experience, great patriotism" that they believed enabled him to protect the nation from its current turmoil in the economic Panic of 1837. Daniel Webster, *Speech Delivered by Daniel Webster at Niblo's Saloon, in New York, on the 15th March, 1837* (New York: Harper, 1837), 1–4.

2. Following the end of the Spanish-American War in 1898, a decision had to be made on what rights the natives of the newly acquired territories would be granted. The initial answer was provided through several court cases that came to be known as the Insular Cases, the most eminent of which was *Downes v. Bidwell*, where the quote is derived. Carman F. Randolph, "The Insular Cases," *Columbia Law Review* 1, no. 7 (1901): 436–40.

3. This victory is in reference to the Anglo-Boer War in which the Boers, or independent Dutch farmers of South Africa, were taken over by the British. Stuart Anderson, "Racial Anglo-Saxonism and the American Response to the Boer War," *Diplomatic History* 2, no. 3 (1978): 219.

4. The concept of the over-soul was coined by Ralph Waldo Emerson (1803-1882) in 1841 as a basic principle of Transcendentalism. According to Emerson, the over-soul is "that great nature in which we rest . . . that Unity within which every man's particular being is contained and made one with all other." Ralph Waldo Emerson, "Essay IX. The Over-Soul," in *Essays, First Series* (Boston: Phillips, Sampson, 1857), 244.

5. "Maud Muller" is the name of a well-known 1856 poem by John Greenleaf Whittier (1807–92), the sentiment of which that is most likely being referenced reads, "Of all sad words of tongue and pen / The saddest are these, 'It might have been.'" John Greenleaf Whittier, *Maud Muller* (Boston: Fields, Osgood, 1870), 12.

MR. BRYAN'S CAMPAIGNS

THE period of American political history between 1896 and 1900 belongs distinctively to Mr. Bryan. When a retrospect shall be taken of it a long time hence he will stand out as the largest figure of all men then living in the United States. Indeed, during these four years he was the most influential individual in the country and none, not excepting Mr. McKinley, occupied a more conspicuous place in the public prints. Scribblers wrote their fingers off making note of his "futility" his "decline," his "rejection;" and found themselves astounded into silence at intervals by his lofty utterances upon the darkening complications that followed the campaign of 1896. Mr. Bryan's luminous influence for good steadily increased after his first defeat[1] and in 1900,[2] appreciative men of insight anticipated one of those recurrences of history, by which a great moral power takes hold of the destinies of a nation. The chilling shock to the ideals of liberty administered by his second defeat can never be fully expressed. Succeeding generations must mature and suffer before they can gather from the words which embodied the people's hope of him, and the words which recorded his loss of the election their deep and painful significance. This, however, is only that concrete failure over which the cynics and satirists of plutocracy have repeated their congratulations. If Mr. Bryan after the campaign of 1900 had compromised his principles, slackened his efforts, or manifested pessimism or ill temper he would have passed into history as another example of a man who lacked moral reserve for the supreme crisis. But he did none of these things. In consequence since 1900 his power has expanded and matured so that he has taken his place as a sort of patriarch, after the fashion of Washington or Jefferson. From this pedestal nothing at all probable can dethrone him. Of what value he is and will be to the country and the world the intuitive mind will not fail to discern.

The democratic platform of 1896 was the molten expression of pent up wrath against evils conterminous with the government itself. The tariff and taxation, bonds and money, the federal courts, the rights of the states are subjects which have occupied political thought in America since the days of Washington. There was nothing novel in this platform and nothing in it to suggest revolutionary designs. There was nothing in it out of harmony with previous platforms of the democratic party. Many of its clauses accorded with platforms of the republican party itself in the days of its beginning. The tempest of villification and mendacity which rose against it can be explained only upon the ground that it was rightly accepted as the sincere declaration of men in sober earnest, who meant exactly what they said and who meant to put their principles into practice if given power to do so. Special privilege was confronted by a powerful and resolute foe, and the best weapons of special privilege, as it turned out, were those things which confused the public memory, prejudiced the public conscience, and subdued the moral energies of the people. The historian who shall depict in comprehensive form that memorable campaign will not fail to note the ardor with which the republican party clasped Mr. Cleveland[3] to its breast because the regenerated democratic party had cast him out, although no one had been more cordially despised by the republican party or more bitterly assailed by its press up to that time. Nor can that historian overlook the organized hypocrisy of the banks, the insurance companies and the monopolies of the country who presented the spectacle of the streets of the great cities of the country gaudily filled with the American flag while the air resounded everywhere with the multitudinous strains of patriotic music for which the monopolists paid the bill. Nothing so brazen and upon such a gigantic scale had ever before been known in this country. It was intended to be a sort of psychical hurricane, by which the people should be swept off their feet in spite of themselves. It very largely helped to accomplish the result that ensued. What was worst the very money which went to the undoing of the people had been taken from them by the wretched swindling of these corporations practiced for at least a third of a century.

The barest reference to history will show that the democratic platform of 1896 proceeded along familiar and creditable lines. Upon the tariff question Mr. Cleveland had been elected president in 1884 and 1892. Free trade or tariff for revenue only had been an article of the democratic faith since the time of Jefferson himself. It was not the tariff plank in the platform which could have honestly excited horror for the "monstrous birth" of the Chicago Convention.[4] As to the income tax our own polity was familiar with such a method of raising revenue. This, therefore, was not strange and forbidding. It was not essentially populistic. The Chicago platform denounced banks of issue.[5] But Jackson[6] was elected president twice because of his opposition to a bank of issue. In this particular then, the platform, fulfilled the requirements of the critics who were clamoring for "historic democracy." There was nothing either novel or improper in the clause of the platform which referred to the Supreme Court and its decision in the income tax case. The republican platform of 1860 contained serious strictures upon the democratic party for using the federal courts to enforce "the extreme pretensions of a purely local interest." It denounced "perversions of judicial power." The platform denounced the sending of troops into Illinois during the railroad strike of 1894[7] in language which was a dilute of similar language in the republican platform of 1860, which referred to the "lawless invasion, by armed force, of the soil of any state or territory as among the worst of crimes." What was here therefore to shock the sensibilities of Mr. McKinley and his party, many of whom had supported the republican platform of 1860? And finally as the republican platform of 1892 had declared for bimetallism, and as Mr. McKinley had vigorously criticized Mr. Cleveland for "dishonoring one of the precious metals;" as the democratic platform of 1892 had declared that "we hold to the use of both gold and silver as the standard money of the country and to the coinage of both gold and silver, without discriminating against either metal" there was nothing in the money plank of the platform of 1896 to alienate any voter unless it inspired the fear that what both parties had up to that time ostensibly favored was on the point of coming to pass.

Somehow in the logic of the world's affairs, resulting perhaps from the power of special privilege and its methods of dissimulation, every trespass upon the rights of man, every reaction toward a discarded injustice can for the time being be set out to masquerade as law or progress. The protective tariff, the national banks, the single gold standard, the great monopolies, the return to militarism and the disregard of the line which divides state from national sovereignty have come to pass through stealth, mendacity and force. It is marvelous, indeed, that any considerable number of men could be made to believe that the readoption of the constitution in its essential form and vigor and the overthrow of these evils was dangerous radicalism or smacked of revolution. If a body of men, like those under John Brown,[8] forcibly assail the "constituted authorities" the offense can be easily designated. If riots occur, if disorder prevails as the result of economic conditions, as a protest against the system, which unjustly distributes to the few wealth beyond their power to use, and to the many less of the means of life than they earn or need, it is still riot and disorder and subject to the courts or the military. Yet a few men who have been able, through one fortune or another, to name the occupants of the several departments of the government, may do infinitely worse things than these and stifle all criticism through the press and the pulpit. This they did in 1896 to an extent never before known except during the time of the war between the states. When special privilege controls the congress, the president and the supreme court no obstacle exists to the passage of any desirable law and to the validation of the law, because it is desirable. But it will require something more than the out-worn jargon of insolent power to persuade reasonable men to believe that that law is sacred, or that an act done in its name is essentially different from an act done without a law, but which is equally violative of the deeper ethical law. So it was in 1896 that men who had taken an oath to support the constitution, but who had maliciously done everything in their power to undermine the republican system, took upon themselves the protection of national honor. The platform of 1896 was denominated revolutionary by those who had themselves revolutionized the government of the United States. To re-establish justice and to re-secure the blessings of liberty were revolutionary ends in the eyes of a party which has established injustice and made the blessings of liberty difficult to ourselves and doubtful to our posterity. Hence it was that Mr. Bryan was assailed in the open and from ambush by every weapon of stupidity, hypocrisy or studied hatred. There was no catch word stimulative of the barbaric prejudices of the mind, which were not raised against him. He not only came through it all unscathed, but with a foresight and wisdom seldom equalled, avoided the snares that plutocracy everywhere spread for his feet.

No man of America, whose capacities we have had a chance to estimate, could have sustained the campaign of 1896 with the ability which Mr. Bryan brought to that trying and laborious task. Neither Jefferson nor Jackson were public speakers of consequence. Both Clay[9] and Webster[10] were impeachable in their private lives; both in fact exhibited vagueness and vacillation of mind on the important subjects of their day. Calhoun[11] entered public life at an early age and had the misfortune to record himself on opposite sides of the same questions. The career of Douglas[12] furnishes its own judgment upon his capacity for the ordeal of 1896. Lincoln was supported by centralism. He found a revolution made to his hands. The foes which he met were a divided democracy, and a special interest weakened by internal strife. Since Lincoln's day and up to the election of Mr. McKinley in 1896, we have produced no man of adaptable ability, who also possessed first rate character. Greeley[13] was not harmoniously consistent. Tilden[14] was vulnerable; so were Garfield,[15] Arthur,[16] Conkling[17] and Blaine.[18] Harrison[19] lacked versatility and magnetism. To consider Mr. McKinley in this connection as having sustained the opposite side of the same campaign the comparison is contemptible. The corrupt treasure of every special privilege in the land was laid at his feet. The railroads delivered crowds at his porch; and instead of making speeches in the midst of arduous travels and after broken rest, he husbanded his strength at home and spoke amidst familiar surroundings and at intervals of repose. Could Mr. Bryan have traveled the length of the land presenting the cause of bimetallism if the opposition could have brought against him any recorded utterance of his in favor of the single gold standard? Could he have faced the hostile sentiment of desperate plutocracy if the "silver mine owners" had paid his debts and rescued him from bankruptcy? Yet Mr. McKinley within less than four years of 1896 had been an ardent bi-metallist. Within the same length of time a rather sinister influence had given him financial assistance of considerable magnitude.

If Mr. Bryan bringing into the political world a light which the world knew not, had been successfully held up as a doubtful character his rejection would have been irrevocable and tragic. But instead, he loosened a current of morality which has flowed to the refreshment of a nation; and is one of the curatives of that awful canker of the soul, whose symptoms have been more pronounced ever since the advent of that hypocrisy which supported Mr. McKinley. Political idealism never had so thorough, so unimpeachable a presentation as it did in the hands of Mr. Bryan during the campaign of 1896. After his convention speech it was apparent that plutocracy was baffled and bewildered. It burst forth into incoherent railings. It then began to conjure with those images which frighten the timorous, confuse the simple, and inspire reflection in the soul of greed. Mr. Bryan was held up as a man who had failed as a lawyer, although no one had ever pretended that Mr. McKinley had succeeded as a lawyer. He was criticised as a man who had made a living out of politics, although he had made a living both as a lawyer and as a newspaper writer, while Mr. McKinley had held office almost without interruption from the time of his majority. At loss at times for something to say his critics found fault with his dress, with the cut of his coat and the style of his collar. Ugly slanders were set afloat in the under-world of gossip in spite of his almost immaculate personal appearance. The plutocratic press scolded and laughed by turns. Orators big and little assailed his political economy in language that frequently showed the grossest ignorance of its simplest principles. He was accused of lacking humor in the face of the fact that Mr. McKinley's habitual stock in trade was a solemn pose. Yet for all that, Mr. Bryan's sallies at Mr. Hanna[20] and his amiable flashes kept the country smiling. The silliness and the inconsistencies which were offered to the public as criticisms of Mr. Bryan showed that the press sometimes successfully maintains a poor regard for the public's sense of the absurd.

Once over the thrilling scare which plutocracy had received, and Mr. McKinley having been made president by the most immoral means outside of a military usurpation, there was observable to political thinkers the laying of plans by which no such other menace to special privilege could be nearly so possible. For the money question was only the strategic point around which the popular forces swarmed in their attack upon special privilege of every sort. Nearly four years after the campaign Congress passed a nominal gold bill; but our fiscal system was not put upon the single gold basis by that law. Before that the coinage of silver dollars had been resumed at the ratio of 16 to 1, thus showing that the republican party was afraid to imperil its lease of power by limiting the country to the single standard. It therefore accepted as correct the quantitative theory of money. The banks came in for favorable legislation in the issue of notes, and a motley combination of provisions were furnished to those chiefly interested, designed to deceive the people, to satisfy the rapacious, and to leave intact that prosperity which was beginning to spring from the energies and favorable situation of the people.

But nevertheless, the centralized grip of monopoly was tightened. It was at once perceived that plutocracy had taken the reins of power, and by cautious and astute degrees was beginning to more thoroughly intrench itself behind the ramparts of the federal government. Powers which had not been exercised by the general government for years were pressed into service, among which was the bankrupt act. Administrative policies indicated the scheme in mind.

Mr. Bryan, undaunted by this defeat, continued his work of education and encouragement. There would have been, in fact, a second battle with the money question as the entering wedge except for the war with Spain. No political party was ever held together by purer enthusiasm or clearer faith than the democratic party after the election of 1896. But an unforeseen fluke in the affairs of the country set Mr. Bryan's plans utterly adrift and gave plutocracy an undreamed of supremacy over the people of America.

Mr. McKinley at first tried to keep the country out of the war. For a moment plutocracy suffered an occultation.[21] It could see only its bonds. Then with swift realization it comprehended greater treasures than the bonds, and greater powers than it had ever known in this country. The democrats in Congress, with an insanity rarely seen, howled themselves hoarse for war and helped plutocracy to forge the first link of militarism and imperialism. They were utterly lost to the thought that the republican party never had anything to offer the people and must either win with a war or upon the memory of a war. And so without any reason whatever the forces of hate and force were turned loose. The viler elements of life were given the supremacy, and those who thirst for power and advantage at any cost broke through the bonds of peace upon missions of "glory." It was a hypocritical war and its fruits have been venomous to the death.

There never was the slightest occasion for debauching our ideals or destroying our institutions. But long ago the spirit of encroachment took courage. At first we had the protective tariff and the bank. Then the supreme court began to usurp powers not given it. Then came the civil war, which unsettled the ideals of liberty. Following upon this were some amazing trespasses upon the organic law. And all the time special privilege was flourishing in an inverse ratio to the destruction of freedom, and was forming over against itself a host of organized discontent. It was this host which made a supreme rally in 1896, perhaps the last to be seen in the country for a long time along old and familiar lines. And it was this host which plutocracy determined, after the election of 1896, to put under foot. The war with Spain[22] furnished the means. It gave an excuse, wicked and hypocritical to be sure, but still an excuse, to begin the organization of a standing army to be used ostensibly to hold and protect our ill-gotten possessions, but in fact and chiefly to cow the labor of the land.

If there was to be a great army there had to be a great navy. Of the same brood came censorship of the press, and in the Philippines the denial of freedom of speech and of trial by jury, those estimable rights hardly ever questioned since the time of William and Mary,[23] and which we could not reserve without the basest treason to principles of liberty which we had proclaimed in a manner none too amiable for more than a hundred years. Government by injunction was greatly strengthened by the change. The suspension of the writ of habeas corpus by a state governor in order more effectually to subjugate labor is now a matter of little moment. Conspiracy prosecutions have become the order of the day. Men are in fact today in America punished for their thoughts and their convictions; and plutocracy brings to the light the skeletons of those who perished in times past under prosecutions which are resurrected as authoritative methods adequate to present conditions of "disorder," "discontent," and even "sedition," a word much used of late. The unfortunate assassination of Mr. McKinley[24] was turned by plutocracy to the greatest account. With this as a pretext the old alien and sedition laws[25] have been revamped only to give them more abhorrent form. These placed in the hands of an executive secretary enable him to arrest any person coming into the country, and to deport the subject without a trial, without witnesses, without a judicial inquiry, and without even a formal accusation. The potentialities of this new law are not known. It may be used against citizens. The twin dragons of imperialism and militarism hatched out by special privilege have inspired in the breasts of thoughtful Americans fears of more tragic days than any we have yet known before they can be slain.

Time must pass before any one can fully judge of Mr. Bryan's course in urging the ratification of the treaty of Paris.[26] It could not be doubted at any time that it meant imperialism. At least, the treaty was so suggestive of imperialism that the chance should not have been taken. Mr. Bryan, nevertheless, for his own sake and for the sake of his party, took prudent grounds in relation to it. He, in fact, was endeavoring to dodge the shadow of the civil war. But it was an awful blunder. One step before him was clear, and that was to oppose the treaty because it was repugnant to the spirit of our peculiar institutions. The next step neither he nor any one else could see. But when the first step is clear in such things the rest must be trusted to that logic of righteousness which is the hope of progress. He justified his course in one of Lincoln's epigrams, but the times were inopportune to quote Lincoln, and the epigram itself was fallacious.[27]

So it was, however, that Mr. Bryan went into the campaign of 1900 without that odium which would have attached to him if he had opposed the treaty and it had been ratified in spite of him. While dealing with the foe he had been with his own country. After the negotiations with the foe were at an end he sought to impress principles of justice and liberty, as well as historic constitutional law, upon the policy toward the islands. There was some political wisdom in this course, and much in it to ward off the attack of the war party. But it was of no real avail. The country had gone too far. Too much had happened to deaden the feelings of the people. The democratic convention of 1900[28] was inspiring to the highest degree, and Mr. Bryan's speech of acceptance placed him on a higher plane as an orator than anything he had ever done. But after their echoes had died away the political atmosphere tingled with a suspicious silence. One hundred years after Thomas Jefferson routed the hosts of centralism and special privilege, imperialism in full armor stepped into power in America, easily brushing aside a man who, in some particulars, is equal to Jefferson himself.

Of a piece with the whole course of insincerity toward Mr. Bryan in the campaign of 1900 were the apologies offered by those who felt conscience stricken for not supporting him. The platform upon which he made the canvass was open to no criticism by those who deplored the Spanish war and its wicked perversions. But Mr. Bryan, in spite of the flattering prophecies of success dinned into his ears if he would abandon the money question, and in spite of appeals from his friends and well-wishers, as well as those who were neither, to abandon it, made the re-affirmation of the money plank in the platform of 1896 a condition of his acceptance of the nomination in 1900. Be this ever said to his credit. Of the many noble things which he did in the four years between 1896 and 1900, no other act of his so much stamped him with greatness and gave him power over the people. If he had renounced the money plank it is true that he would have fallen into the hands of those who wanted to make him out a mere figurante[29] of the day with an overweening ambition for place. But still those enemies, if disposed to be consistent, should have admitted that the plank made no difference, because the gold standard had become the settled law, and Mr. Bryan could not have changed it during his term if elected, owing to the complexion of the Senate. This was the unctuous[30] self-gratulation of the organs of the republican party until Mr. Bryan compelled the re-affirmation of the platform of 1896. Now suddenly a great outcry was made that the gold standard would be threatened by his election, and that body of men who knew that Mr. McKinley's election meant imperialism, and who had opposed the imperial policy of his administration, faced about pretendedly because the money question was more important than the question of imperialism—the money question of whose settlement beyond Mr. Bryan's power, if elected, to disturb, they had rejoiced and boasted!

This is a cursory outline of the record which the republican party made between 1896 and 1900, and of the record which Mr. Bryan and his party made. No human power can add to or take away from either record. In time to come both records will be known and compared, and every writing and fact necessary to their clear understanding will be brought to light. There will be no doubt at the seat of judgment which controls the verdicts of history in what manner those records shall be judged. For the open and secret deeds of those will be known who "blew out the moral lights around us,"[31] and left a great nation fashioned after the purest and most philosophic principles of idealism to flounder in darkness and mire.

Notes

1. William Jennings Bryan first ran for president in 1896, losing to William McKinley by 271 electoral votes to 176.

2. In 1900, Bryan was again the Democratic nominee for president but fared worse against McKinley's reelection effort, losing by an electoral count of 292 to 155. David J. Silbey. *A War of Frontier and Empire: The Philippine-American War, 1899–1902* (New York: Hill and Wang, 2007), 160.

3. Grover Cleveland (1837-1908) was governor of New York and then the twenty-second and twenty-fourth president (1885–89, 1893–97). He was the first Democrat to be elected president since James Buchanan in 1856 and would be the last until Woodrow Wilson in 1912.

4. Masters is referring to the 1896 Democratic Convention, where William Jennings Bryan was nominated for president and gave his "Cross of Gold" speech. Jackson Lears, *Rebirth of a Nation: The Making of Modern America, 1877–1920*. (New York: Harper Perennial, 2010), 186–87.

5. Banks of issue are founded by governments to issue banknotes. Andrew Jackson vetoed a charter renewal for the Second Bank of the United States in 1832, leaving state banks in control of the nation's cash reserves. See Robert Remini, *Andrew Jackson and the Bank War: A Study in the Growth of Presidential Power* (New York: W. W. Norton, 1967).

6. Andrew Jackson (1767–1845) was the seventh president (1829–37) and is widely considered the founder of the Democratic Party.

7. A strike at the Pullman Car Company just outside of Chicago began on May 11 and spread throughout the country. Federal intervention broke the strike by mid-July.

8. John Brown (1800–59) was an abolitionist from Connecticut known for his guerrilla attacks in Kansas and the 1859 raid on the federal arsenal at Harpers Ferry, Virginia.

9. Henry Clay (1777–1852) was a senator, a representative, and the Speaker of the House from Kentucky who served as secretary of state under John Quincy Adams.

10. Daniel Webster was a representative and senator from Massachusetts who also served as secretary of state from 1841 to 1843 before returning to the Senate.

11. John C. Calhoun was a representative from South Carolina who served as secretary of war from 1817 to 1825 and was twice elected vice president. After resigning the vice presidency in 1832, he was elected to the Senate, where he served until his death. Throughout his career, Calhoun was an advocate for states' rights and a defender of the rights of enslavers.

12. Stephen A. Douglas (1813–61) was a representative and senator from Illinois who was the 1860 Democratic nominee for president.

13. Horace Greeley (1811–72) was the founder and editor of the *New York Tribune*, a representative, and the 1872 Democratic nominee for president.

14. Samuel Tilden (1814–86) was governor of New York and the 1876 Democratic nominee for president. The election was decided by congressional committee and awarded to Rutherford B. Hayes.

15. James Garfield (1831–81) was a representative from Ohio who was elected as the twentieth president in 1880. He was shot in July 1881, dying from his wound in September of the same year.

16. Chester A. Arthur (1829–86) was Garfield's vice president and became the twenty-first president upon Garfield's death.

17. Roscoe Conkling (1829–88) was a representative and senator from New York and head of the state Republican Party.

18. James G. Blaine (1830–93) was a representative from Maine who served as Speaker of the House from 1869 to 1875, senator from 1876 to 1881, and secretary of state to Garfield, Arthur, and Harrison. He was a multiple-time presidential candidate.

19. Benjamin Harrison (1833–1901) was a senator from Indiana and was elected as the twenty-third president in 1888. He both defeated and lost to Grover Cleveland.

20. Mark Hanna (1837–1904) was a senator from Ohio who was an influential supporter of the Hayes, Garfield, and McKinley presidential campaigns.

21. "The state of being hidden from view or lost to notice." *Webster's Practical Dictionary*, s.v. "occultation."

22. The Spanish-American War began after the USS *Maine* exploded on February 15, 1898, in Cuba. War was officially declared on April 25, 1898, leading to the Philippine-American War. A treaty ending the war was signed December 10, 1898. Silbey, *War of Frontier and Empire*, 33–34, 58.

23. William of Orange and Queen Mary II of England (1662–94). They rose to power after deposing Queen Mary's father, King James II.

24. William McKinley was shot by Leon Czolgosz, an anarchist, on September 6, 1901, while visiting the Pan-American Exposition in New York. He died on September 14, leading to Theodore Roosevelt being sworn in as president of the United States. Silbey, *War of Frontier and Empire*, 187–88.

25. The Alien and Sedition Acts of 1798 made it illegal to "print, utter, or publish… any false, scandalous, and malicious" material against the government.

26. Masters is referring to the 1898 treaty that ended the Spanish-American War. Silbey, *War of Frontier and Empire*, 56, 65.

27. Masters here refers to Bryan's speech at the 1900 Democratic Convention, in which he states, "For a time, Republican leaders were inclined to deny to opponents the right to criticize the Philippine policy of the administration, but upon investigation they found that both Lincoln and Clay asserted and exercised the right to criticize a President during the progress of the Mexican war."

28. The convention was held in Kansas City, and Bryan was nominated by unanimous vote on the first ballot.

29. The female form of figurant, here meaning "an accessory character to the stage, who figures in its scenes, but has nothing to say." *Webster's Practical Dictionary*, s.v. "figurante."

30. "Fat; oily; greasy." *Webster's Practical Dictionary*, s.v. "unctuous."

31. This quote is from Lincoln's speech at the Galesburg Debate on October 7, 1858.

Observations on
Democracy

AFTER a century of insidious slander of democracy the American people as a mass are beginning to show a confused conception of the ideals of free institutions. To say that the people are too zealous of their own welfare to relinquish any substantial right is to utter a fine phrase and ignore the facts. They have already parted with substantial rights; they continue to part with them and new propositions to surrender others are met by united acquiescence and divided protest. The policy of giving state aid to the mercantilists and taxing all others to do it;[1] of fondling the producer and smiting the consumer; of considering capital as something to be worshiped and labor as something quite common, quite as a matter of fact and quite subsidiary to capital, has brought its logical result at last. In spite of philosophy, in spite of its interpreters in the persons of our most distinguished statesmen; in spite of the examples and teachings of the fathers and the warnings of their faithful successors, and in spite of sad experiences of other people at other times; in spite of all that should have curbed the spirit so reactionary to the policy of a republic, the American people today find themselves bewildered over principles which no one assailed a generation ago.

For along with this repression and favoritism there has accumulated in the hands of a few great wealth and great power. These influences instruct the young; they mould history and write it after it is moulded; they exalt and dethrone at will; they crown mediocrity and strike down merit; they have monopolized the means of intelligence; the girdles and the highways which circle the globe are theirs; the widow's oil and the farmer's salt are theirs; they have stolen all the weapons of caricature, satire and argument. And they have rapidly created a public sentiment which favors everything except the peccadilloes.[2] The school histories, the accessible biographies are written with a view of prejudicing the young against popular institutions. Jefferson, Madison and Jackson are belittled in order to make room for the magnification of Hamilton and Marshall. With no patron saints but an astute bookkeeper and a complaisant[3] judge they have enthroned themselves and demand attention. They fill the air with chattering panegyric over men who hated republican principles.

The important work of Jefferson, the most important ever performed by any statesman, which belongs not merely to the lower world of statecraft but has pierced into the rarer realm of philosophy, has been assaulted at its base for years, indoctrinating successive generations with a spirit of hatred for the memory of him whom the Olympus of judgment has placed above all Americans. And what is Jefferson charged with? Listen: Jefferson was not a warrior; he was a coward; he wrote anonymous letters; he did not walk straight; he did not look one in the eye. On the other hand Hamilton was a soldier; he was brave; he acknowledged his productions; he held his head erect; his piercing glance abashed the most self-possessed. But it is not considered that he devised an anonymous system of indirect taxation, by which the earnings of one man can be transferred to the pockets of another man, pursuant to which the evils of today have largely come to pass. If Jefferson wrote the "Anas,"[4] Hamilton fathered the protective tariff which nearly everyone has discovered is a deception; if Jefferson did not walk erect, if he did not look his hearer in the eye, Hamilton planned to revolutionize the republic and to do it by subterfuge and chicane.

In this unequal struggle, unequal for fifty years at least, the ideals of democracy have ceased to present themselves clearly to the eyes of the American people. In the lust for wealth and power officials have forgotten that they are not in office for themselves, but for the people. General corruption has undermined faith in the administration of the law. This condition of feeling is very responsive to arguments of absolutism. How close we are to that now time alone can determine. But that there is a silent sentiment for it, especially in those portions of the country which fought democracy with the Hartford convention and by good luck expunged their infamy through this traduction[5] already discussed, there can be no doubt.

What, then, of democracy do we hold fast to? Is it man's equality? But that is attacked, not by denying what it means, that all men have equal rights be-before the law, but by saying that all men are not equal, because men differ in mental power and character, which it does not mean. Then it follows that every proposition of democracy must be again defended. All is upset which we thought secure. All is confusion where once was order. All that was done must be done again. A spirit of rude iconoclasm has swept over from the middle ages, and masquerading as progress goes about to tear down what was built so firmly centuries ago.

Do governments derive their just powers from the consent of the governed? That was once the general tenet in this country. But now it is disputed. It is now held that there is a metaphysical substance called sovereignty not derived from the people, but which proceeds from the same source that originates the sovereignty of despotism, and is the same thing in degree and kind. It is the child of destiny and the voice of God. It is the recrudescence[6] of Philip's[7] power and it may send its duke of Alva[8] anywhere in the world to subdue heresy and cow rebellion.

Is liberty an inalienable right? Yes, but—! It may be so, but—! Liberty, why of course, but—! Liberty must be carefully circumscribed or it will spread into license.

Is the pursuit of happiness an inalienable right? This is impugned by all our modern legislation. The government has surrendered to a marauding band of giant monopolies the sovereign power of taxation. For the power to destroy competition, and in its turn to fix prices at will, is an exercise of the taxing power, while every dollar taken from a man decreases his liberty to pursue his own way in life and weakens his capacity as a citizen. For along with such perversion of justice there is born the spirit of anarchy on one side and of socialism on the other; anarchy, which would uproot all government, and socialism, which would make government of everything. And as discontent is heard in the land the only remedy suggested is the club, not to destroy the injustice, but to beat down discontent with the injustice. Thus we have government by injunction and expediency in legislation.

But democracy itself has been at fault. As a matter of fact, there is no such thing as traditional democracy; it has no historic character to which the democratic party of today can turn for guidance. The democratic party has been for free trade and then for protection. It was on both sides of the bank question; it opposed and championed internal improvements. It was for hard money and it worshiped at the shrine of the greenback. And while its several opposing parties were equally vacillating it was natural that they should be so. They were seeking at all times to draw the government into the hands of a few men, which was a difficult process; while to keep the government in the hands of the people as a means to democratic ends was generally a popular creed. It found general acceptance and it should have been the objective point at all times.

The principles of democracy, therefore, cannot always be found in its platforms. All of its tenets can be deduced from the great outlines of the declaration of independence. They were written there out of the fullness of the human heart; their inspiration was the necessary logic of human life. What each desires are life and liberty and the privilege to seek his own; to have that which he earns and to surrender none of it to others under the law except what is necessary to protect others in the same enjoyment. It is in the human heart that democracy has erected her temple; it is from the human heart that the voice of democracy, whether in grief or joy, whether subdued or victorious, ever speaks and will speak forever.

But to emphasize the rights of the common people, as if democracy was concerned alone with them, is an erroneous and pernicious course. Democracy concerns itself with no class. It demands that the poor man shall have and enjoy his own; that he shall worship and speak and act as he pleases up to the limit of the same right as every other man.

Whoever by diligence has acquired wealth shall also enjoy and keep what he has gained. Children, even, shall inherit idleness from him who earned it. The end of democracy is not the rule of the common people. The end of democracy is the development of the individual in intellect and morals and usefulness, in a sense of justice, in the virtues of the heart, and to that end democracy demands liberty, and to obtain liberty it reposes the government in the whole people. If there be failure, which is minimized by popular rule, it is by the same token guaranteed a speedy and comprehensive amendment. Democracy believes in wealth for all who can by industry and intelligence obtain it. It will not permit trespass or confiscation. Nor will it by special privilege from the state suffer a part to acquire wealth at the expense of the many. Such a course impugns the principle of man's equality, which is the first clause in its creed.

Democracy demands freedom of conscience. It was won by the most painful struggle in the history of man. Nor is it in these days of unsettled ideals very generally assailed. While Charles V[9] reasoned that there was but one religion and one salvation, and that to punish heresy was to serve God and man, no one now fails to smile at this quaint sophistry. It passed away long ago where a great deal else that still lingers to hamper mankind should have gone.

As a principle of government democracy demands the least government consistent with public order and the general welfare. It limits its interference to trespasses. Whenever a hand is uplifted or a plot, concocted to assail equal rights, democracy enters its effectual protest. And in the observance of this simple rule is a great reward to the people as a whole. Under its benign influence there are no boards to intermeddle in private affairs; there is no corrupt officialism; there is little chance for powerful machines; there is frugality in administrations; there are no useless and costly navies; there no standing armies; there is no extravagant flummery; there is no grabbing of a scrubby island, and then of other islands to protect the first; there are no subsidies, no protective tariffs, no system of finance which favors a part of the people; no public debt, and, in short, none of the numberless devices which are foisted upon the people whether they will or no, upon pretenses good or bad, inventions of the Medicis[10] and the Machiavellians[11] of history who worked the incantations of power and glory in benighted times. But they are worked today, for one of the strange paradoxes in the political thought of the masses is the pride and satisfaction which they manifest in granting to a central body far away the very power by which their rights are admittedly infringed.

It follows from what has been said that the components of democracy are the free city, the free township, the free county and the free state, co-operating in a synthetic process to the national government. This is the ideal of democracy. There can be no republic without it. Our fathers learned the lesson from the free cities of Italy and the Netherlands, and the truth of local self-government is so obvious that the very statementof the proposition exhausts explanation and comment. And in good report and ill, in spite of falsehood and sophistry, the democracy has adhered to this principle. There never was a time when democratic leaders were not in favor of a nation, although there was honest difference of opinion as to the powers of the nation. But the process to which democracy was ever and ever will be a remorseless foe is the accumulation of all power in the hands of a few men, which was the hobby of Hamilton and which in our day has almost come to pass.

And as inclusive of all that has been defined democratic government extends to the enforcement of the law of equal freedom. It is a simple policy. It does not abound in promises of favors; it only insures justice. It does not appeal to the vision in glorious pageants; it convinces the intellect by its logic; it warms the heart by its humanity. It does not symbolize itself in serried ranks of armed men, through which the ruler rides amidst the plaudits of those who claw the cap from the peaked head, while women weep and strong men faint with emotion at the sight of God-given power. It parades no squadron of battleships before the blurred eyes of sycophants and sentimentalists. It cares nothing for tinsel and finery, for black robes and wigs, for that mummery and pretense which is practiced to overawe the sentiments of those who are in the humble walks of life and convince them that its functions are intrusted[12] to the anointed, and that those who are predestined to service and labor must obey implicitly and pay entirely.

But what is the symbol of democracy? It is the carpenter, the mechanic, the boatman, the shoemaker, the farmer, the tradesman, the banker, the lawyer, the philosopher, each in his way of life doing the world's work, protected by his own government in his rightful liberty, and in the aggregate mass of robust justice and honorable strength reserving a power for perpetuation which only internal corruption can destroy. Its apparel is that of Lincoln, and its surroundings are the books and the hospitality of Jefferson—things which do not cloud the eyes or enslave the feelings, but which in their simple majesty and merit are the enduring and beneficent pictures of history.

It follows that what is the strength of democracy is its weakness. It does not promise something for nothing; it does not argue that to take from one part and add to the other part increases the bulk of the whole; that to tax the many for the few enriches all; that to subsidize a private enterprise is profitable to those who are interested only in paying the subsidy; that wealth can be created by taxation; that to pay interest on a large and growing public debt is beneficial to the people; that a surplus locked up in the treasury drawn by taxation is a sign of prosperity—none of those things does it pretend, promise or preach. It offers nothing but equal freedom to all. To those who want more democracy is not attractive; upon those who are deceived into taking less its warnings are lost. For the malevolent side of life shadows every virtue with a fault. And no question can be so fairly, so clearly stated that ingenious sophistry will not give it an evil aspect.

To instance this let us take a few examples from history. Those who opposed and oppose the tariff are in favor of pauper labor; they are inimical[13] to American industry; they believe in a cheap man and a cheap coat; those who struggle against centralization in government are loose in their morals; they are not in favor of order and law; those who decry the subjugation of feeble peoples and the taking of their country are cowards; they are weaklings; they are behind the times; they are disloyal, unpatriotic; they are rebels at heart, the offshoots of impotent treason in days past. Groundless as are these charges, aimless and foolish as they are, they are preferred on a deep and astute principle, viz., that men must rely for their guidance on what is said by men who talk and editors who write, that the majority of men cannot personally investigate these questions and that reiteration of these calumnies[14] will instill a spirit of skepticism of the best motives and the purest professions. This course is as old as the discussion of public questions. It is the warfare of vile debate, through which humanity drags its feet by difficult steps or from which humanity staggers back into the shadows of a perished century.

Finally, democracy is intensely practical. It has no refined and protracted problems to solve, such as afflict the system of socialism. It need not concern itself with how property shall be first divided and afterward how it shall be kept in a condition of equality; how many hours men shall work; what they shall eat if they do work or what if they do not; what schooling shall be maintained. It has no devious course of idealism to trace out and explore before it can set to work, and no unforeseen steps to trust to luck, beyond the limits of forethought.

Democracy outlines her program in a few simple words: Men shall enjoy liberty of action up to the limit of the same liberty for all men; there shall be equal freedom; he who infringes this rule shall be punished. Under this benign system democracy knows that humanity will progress, because the individual must develop. It is not a prophecy, but a fact. The state neither adds to nor takes from the law of the survival of the fittest. The task of mitigating that law it leaves to man in his private life, in his condition of untrammeled strength which results from freedom. To what end shall there be special privilege? To what end shall a class be created or an aristocracy of wealth or prerogative established? How often has the aristocracy produced men who furnished humanity with philosophy, invention, discovery or statesmanship? And whenever an aristocracy has produced such men how have they risen to real greatness except by following with more or less faithfulness the principle of liberty?

Democracy draws no long face about charity, nor does it whine about love. Democracy is content with justice, which is practicable and which the state can and ought to enforce. No amount of preaching can make men love each other, and involuntary charity, such as the state sometimes commands, leads to extensive abuse. State charity covers from the eyes of the people a multitude of political sins. Democracy nourishes the feelings of individual worth and cultivates proper pride. It abhors the snob and the lackey. Founded upon freedom, it has no cause to serve except humanity. It owes no personal fealty. It cares nothing for that patriotism which consists in cringing adoration of an administration. It is indifferent to the flag when it degenerates into a piece of gorgeous bunting and no longer represents anything but force.

Whatever is independent, progressive and self-reliant in Americans, whatever in them is noble and just, they owe to democracy. It is democracy that makes them demand their rights and insist on fair play for all. It is democracy that keeps the way open for the unbounded energy of Americans. It is democracy that laughs at cant[15] and slaps the solemn jowls of hypocrisy. It is the hard head of democracy that refuses to be turned by pompous silliness and that scoffs at pretense. It is democracy that gives sincerity to life and its endeavors. It is democracy that is regardless of a man's purse or his clothes, but looks to his mind, his virtues and his manners. It is democracy that respects the toiler, whether he toil with his hands or with his brains. It is democracy that believes in the aristocracy of ability and morality and is glad to see a frock coat on the back of any man who has earned it. It is democracy that is subduing the hands which are opposing it, that is bringing freedom of trade to America, and by slow but sure processes is establishing all it has contended for—while these ideas, which are not for an age, but for all time so long as the world is as it is, are progressing to the uttermost parts of the globe.

Notes

1. To raise revenue and protect domestic industries, the federal government imposed heavy tariffs on foreign goods. The cost of the tariff was passed on to the consumers who purchased these goods. Orrin Leslie Elliott, *The Tariff Controversy in the United States, 1789–1833* (Charleston, SC: Nabu Press, 2012), 19.

2. "A slight trespass or offense; a petty crime or fault." *Webster's Practical Dictionary*, s.v. "peccadillo."

3. "Desirous to please; kindly attentive; courteous; well-bred." *Webster's Practical Dictionary*, s.v. "complaisant."

4. "Anas" refers to Jefferson's compilation of notes and memoranda from his time as secretary of state and president. See Thomas Jefferson, *The Complete Anas of Thomas Jefferson*, ed. Franklin Sawvel (New York: Round Table Press, 1903).

5. "Derivation from one of the same kind; propagation; transmission from one to another." *Webster's Practical Dictionary*, s.v. "traduction."

6. "Increased severity of a disease after temporary remission." *Webster's Complete Dictionary of the English Language* (1886), 1099, s.v. "recrudescence."

7. Philip II was king of Spain from 1556 until his death and used Spanish power to expand Catholic influence in Europe and the New World. See J. H. Elliot, *Imperial Spain: 1469–1716* (London: Penguin Books, 1963, 2002).

8. Fernando Alvarez de Toledo y Pimentel, Duke of Alva (1507–82), was a Spanish general sent to the Netherlands by Philip II in 1567 to end the rebellion against Spanish rule. See Henry Kamen, *The Duke of Alva* (New Haven, CT: Yale University Press, 2004).

9. Charles V (1500–58) was king of Spain and Holy Roman emperor at the height of Spanish power in Europe and in the Americas. See Harald Kleinschmidt, *Charles V: The World Emperor* (Stroud, UK: Sutton, 2004).

10. The Medicis were a banking family that ruled Florence from the fifteenth to the eighteenth centuries and used their wealth to wield influence across Europe. See Ferdinand Schevill, *History of Florence: From the Founding of the City through the Renaissance* (New York: Frederick Ungar, 1976).

11. "Pertaining to Machiavelli, an Italian writer, or to his supposed principles; politically cunning; using duplicity; crafty." *Webster's Practical Dictionary*, s.v. "Machiavellian."

12. Alternate spelling of the word entrusted.

13. "Having the disposition or temper of an enemy; unfriendly." *Webster's Complete Dictionary of the English Language*(1886) s.v. "inimical."

14. "False accusation; defamation; slander." *Webster's Practical Dictionary*, s.v. "calumny."

15. "An affected mode of speaking; a word or phrase hackneyed, corrupt, or peculiar to some profession." *Webster's Practical Dictionary*, s.v. "cant."

CONTRIBUTORS

APPENDIX

SELECTED BIBLIOGRAPHY

INDEX

CONTRIBUTORS

Brandon Adams is a PhD student at Southern Illinois University Edwardsville. His focus is on the study of hegemony within the historical narrative.

Scott Both is an alumni of Southern Illinois University Edwardsville, with both a MA in historical studies, a BS in history, and a minor in political science. His interest is in eighteenth- and nineteenth-century US history, military, politics, and religion.

Joseph Davis is a history major who plans to go into secondary education. He is especially interested in Illinois history and is currently student teaching at Collinsville High School.

Shawn Emily is a MA candidate at Southern Illinois University Edwardsville. His focus is antebellum America and the Gilded Age.

Jessica Guldner is an alumni of Murray State University currently pursuing a master's in history at Southern Illinois University Edwardsville with an emphasis in US history and social history. She holds a BA in history with a minor in religious studies.

Amy Kapp is an undergraduate history student at Southern Illinois University Edwardsville. She is especially interested in art and community-focused history.

Joseph King is an undergraduate history major student at Southern Illinois University Edwardsville. He is interested in twentieth-century US history and animation history.

Andrew Niederhauser is a PhD student at Southern Illinois University Edwardsville. His focus is on queer history and sexuality in the early American republic.

Abbigayle Schaefer is a student in the museum studies program at Southern Illinois University Edwardsville. She specializes in public and applied history and is especially interested in local and community-focused historical projects.

Elizabeth Schroader is an undergraduate English student at Southern Illinois University Edwardsville. She plans to go into library science.

Andrew Shepherd is an undergraduate history major student at Southern Illinois University Edwardsville who plans to pursue a master's in history. He is interested in Native American history and twentieth-century US history.

Jason Stacy is a professor of history at Southern Illinois University Edwardsville. He is interested in nineteenth-century US history, pedagogy, and documentary editing.

Nicholas Swain is an undergraduate history student at Southern Illinois University Edwardsville. He is particularly interested in nineteenth-century US history.

Lucas Turnbull is a undergraduate history major student at Southern Illinois University Edwardsville. He is interested in world history from the ancient world to the Middle Ages.

Appendix
Biographical Directory of Major Figures Mentioned

John Adams (1735–1826), first vice president of the United States (1789–97) and consecutively the second president (1797–1801), was an important member of the Continental Congress and one of the signers of the Declaration of Independence. His work *Thoughts on Government* (1776) influenced how many of the original thirteen colonies wrote their state constitutions.

Samuel Adams (1722–1803) fought for American independence in the Continental Congress and was also one of the signers of the Declaration of Independence. He went on to become governor of Massachusetts (1794–97).

Augustus Caesar (63 BCE–14 CE) was the first Roman emperor. His reign was the height of Roman power and introduced an era of peace known as the Pax Romana (27 BCE–180 CE).

Henry Billings Brown (1836–1913) was an associate justice of the U.S. Supreme Court (1890–1906). He wrote the majority decision in the *Plessy v. Ferguson* case (1896), which established that state-mandated segregation laws did not violate the equal protection clause of the 14th Amendment.

William Jennings Bryan (1860–1925) was a representative from Nebraska (1891–95), three-time failed presidential candidate (1896, 1900, 1908), and secretary of state under Woodrow Wilson (1913–15). He was a populist Democrat who championed many ideas that eventually became law, such as direct election of senators and women's suffrage.

John C. Calhoun (1782–1850) was a representative and senator from South Carolina who served as secretary of war (1817–25) and was twice elected vice president (1824, 1828). He was the leading congressional advocate for state sovereignty and the rights of slaveholders.

Grover Cleveland (1837–1908) was governor of New York and then the twenty-second and twenty-fourth president (1885–89, 1893–97). He was the first Democrat to be elected president since James Buchanan in 1856 (1857–61) and would be the last until Woodrow Wilson in 1912.

Benjamin Franklin (1706–90) helped draft the Declaration of Independence and served as ambassador to France (1779–85). He was also a well-known scientist, printer, and polymath.

Alexander Hamilton (1757–1804) authored fifty-one of the eighty-five Federalist Papers and was instrumental in the creation and ratification of the U.S. Constitution. He was the first secretary of the Treasury (1789–95) and worked to establish the public credit system, national banks, tariffs, and the U.S. Mint.

Patrick Henry (1736–99) served as the first and sixth governor of Virginia (1776–79, 1784–86). He was an Anti-Federalist whose opposition to the ratification of the Constitution helped lead to the creation of the Bill of Rights.

Andrew Jackson (1767–1845) was the seventh president of the United States (1829–37) and one of the founders of the Democratic Party. He was a supporter of states' rights and the expansion of slavery into the western United States. He also passed the Indian Removal Act (1830).

John Jay (1745–1829) was the first chief justice of the U.S. Supreme Court (1789–95) and governor of New York (1795–1801) and negotiated Jay's Treaty (1794), which settled major economic grievances with Great Britain and promoted commercial prosperity. He also authored five of the Federalist Papers with James Madison and Alexander Hamilton.

Thomas Jefferson (1743–1826) was the third president of the United States (1801–9) and the primary author of the Declaration of Independence. During his presidency, he doubled the size of the country with the Louisiana Purchase (1803).

James Madison (1751–1836) was the fourth president of the United States (1809–17). He authored twenty-nine of the Federalist Papers and was instrumental in the creation and ratification of the U.S. Constitution and Bill of Rights. Allied with Thomas Jefferson against Alexander Hamilton's national bank, Madison served as Jefferson's secretary of state and oversaw the Louisiana Purchase. While president, he led the United States during the War of 1812, which lasted until 1815.

John Marshall (1755–1835) was the fourth chief justice of U.S. Supreme Court (1801–35). Marshall is most known for presiding over the *Marbury v. Madison* case (1803), which established the Supreme Court's power of judicial review.

William McKinley (1843–1901) was the twenty-fifth president of the United States and the last to serve in the Civil War (1861–65). He led the country during the Spanish-American War (1898), raised protective tariffs to boost American industry, and kept the nation on the gold standard.

John Stuart Mill (1806–73) was an English philosopher and member of Parliament (1865–68), most famous for his works *Utilitarianism* (1863), which promotes the belief that the right course of action is one that does the most good, and *On Liberty* (1859), which focuses on the relationship between social authority and the liberty of the individual.

Theodore Roosevelt (1858–1919) was governor of New York (1899–1900), assistant secretary of the navy (1897–98), vice president (1901), and twenty-sixth president of the United States (1901–9) after the assassination of William McKinley. He was a progressive, as well as an imperialist, who focused on making America a world power.

Adam Smith (1723–90) was a philosopher most famously known as the father of modern capitalism for his work *An Inquiry into the Nature and Causes of the Wealth of Nations* (1776).

Joseph Story (1779–1845) was an associate justice of the U.S. Supreme Court (1812–45) who was most famous for his majority opinion in *United States v. Schooner Amistad* (1841), where he argued that the people who revolted on the *Amistad* were wrongly enslaved and therefore free. His legal philosophy was aligned with John Marshall and Alexander Hamilton.

Roger B. Taney (1777–1864) was the fifth chief justice of the U.S. Supreme Court (1836–64). He is most known for his majority opinion in *Dred Scott v. Sanford* (1857), where he argued that constitutional rights did not extend to African Americans.

Selected Bibliography

Primary Sources

Bouvier, John. *A Law Dictionary, Adapted to the Constitution and Laws.* Philadelphia: J. B. Lippincott, 1883.

Bryce, James. *The American Commonwealth.* 3 vols. London: Macmillan, 1888.

Camp, David N., ed. *The American Year-Book and National Register for 1869.* Vol. 1. Hartford: O. D. Case, 1869.

Cheyney, Edward P. "The Court of Star Chamber." *American Historical Review* 18, no. 4 (1913): 727–50.

Cooley, Thomas M. *A Treatise on the Constitutional Limitations: Which Rest upon the Legislative Power of the States of the American Union.* Boston: Little, Brown, 1868.

Elliot, Jonathan, ed. *The Debates in the Several State Conventions on the Adoption of the Federal Constitution as Recommended by the General Convention at Philadelphia in 1787.* 2nd ed. 5 vols. Washington, D.C.: Taylor and Maury, 1836–59.

Emerson, Ralph Waldo. "Essay IX. The Over-Soul." In *Essays, First Series,* 243–70. Boston: Phillips, Sampson, 1857.

Hamilton, Alexander. *Alexander Hamilton's Famous Report on Manufactures.* Boston: Home Market Club, 1892.

———. "Hamilton's Opinion as to the Constitutionality of the Bank of the United States." In *The Federalist: A Commentary on the Constitution of the United States by Alexander Hamilton, James Madison, and John Jay.* Edited by Paul Leicester Ford, 655–78. New York: Henry Holt, 1898.

———. *The Papers of Alexander Hamilton: From Alexander Hamilton to John Jay.* Harold C. Syrett., New York: Columbia University Press, 1976.

Hart, Albert Bushnell, and Edward Channing, eds. *The Virginia and Kentucky Resolutions: With the Alien, Sedition, and Other Acts, 1798–1799.* New York: Parker P. Simmons, 1912.

Jefferson, Thomas, *The Complete Anas of Thomas Jefferson.* Edited by Franklin Sawvel. New York: Round Table Books, 1903.

Lawrence, T. J. *Essays on Some Disputed Questions in Modern International Law.* London: George Bell and Sons, 1884.

———. *A Handbook of Public International Law.* London: George Bell and Sons, 1890.

———. *The Principles of International Law.* Boston: D. C. Heath, 1895.

Lindsey, William. *John Marshal Day 1801–1901 Centennial Proceedings of the Chicago Bar February 4, 1901.* Chicago: Hollister Brothers, 1901.

Lodge, Henry Cabot. *Alexander Hamilton.* Boston: Houghton, 1882.

Marshall, John. *The Writings of John Marshall: Late Chief Justice of the United States, upon the Federal Constitution.* Washington, D.C.: William H. Morrison, 1890.

Masters, Edgar Lee. *Across Spoon River: An Autobiography.* New York: Farrar and Rinehart, 1936.

———. *Across Spoon River: An Autobiography.* Urbana and Chicago, IL: Univesity of Illinois Press, 1991.

———. *The Blood of the Prophets.* Chicago: Rook Press, 1905.

———. *Lincoln: The Man.* New York: Dodd, Mead, 1931.

———. *Spoon River Anthology.* New York: Macmillan, 1915.

Morris, Gouverneur. *The Diary and Letters of Gouverneur Morris.* Vol. 2. Edited by Anne Cary Morris. New York: Charles Scribner's Sons, 1888.

Randolph, Carman F. "The Insular Cases." *Columbia Law Review* 1, no. 7 (1901): 436–70.

Robertson, J. A. "The Effect in the Philippines of the Senate 'Organic Act.'" *Journal of Race Development* 6, no. 4 (1916): 370–87.

Seward, William H. *The Works of William H. Seward.* Vol. 1. Edited by George E. Baker. New York: Redfield, 1853.

Story, Joseph. *Commentaries of the Constitution of the United States; with a Preliminary Review of the Constitutional History of the Colonies and States, before the Adoption of the Constitution.* Vol. 2. Boston: Hillard, Gray, 1833.

Thornton, William Wheeler, ed. *The Universal Cyclopaedia of Law: A Practical Compendium of Legal Information.* 2 vols. Long Island: Edward Thompson, 1885.

Walker, Timothy. *Introduction to American Law: Designed as a First Book for Students.* 6th ed. Boston: Little, Brown, 1874.

Webster, Daniel. *Speech Delivered by Daniel Webster at Niblo's Saloon, in New York, on the 15th March, 1837.* New York: Harper, 1837.

Whittier, John Greenleaf. *Maud Muller.* Boston: Fields, Osgood, 1870.

SECONDARY SOURCES

Adams, Henry. *The Second Administration of Thomas Jefferson.* New York: Scribner, 1921.

Anderson, Stuart. "Racial Anglo-Saxonism and the American Response to the Boer War." *Diplomatic History* 2, no. 3 (1978): 219–36.

Baker, John H. *An Introduction to English Legal History.* Oxford: Oxford University Press, 2019.

Bassiry, G. R., and Marc Jones. "Adam Smith and the Ethics of Contemporary Capitalism." *Journal of Business Ethics* 12, no. 8 (1993): 621–27.

Boyer, Richard E. "English Declarations of Indulgence of 1687 and 1688." *Catholic Historical Review* 50, no. 3 (1964): 332–71.

Brunello, Anthony R. "The Madisonian Republic and Modern Nationalist Populism: Democracy and the Rule of Law." *World Affairs* 181, no. 2 (2018): 106–32.

Burton, David H. "Theodore Roosevelt: Confident Imperialist." *Review of Politics* 23, no. 3 (1961): 356–77.

Champlin, Edward. "Nero Reconsidered." *New England Review* 19, no. 2 (1998): 97–108.

Cherny, Robert W. *A Righteous Cause: The Life of William Jennings Bryan.* Norman: University of Oklahoma Press, 1994.

Clark, Peter. *Henry Hallam.* Boston: Twayne, 1982.

Corwin, Edward S. "The Passing of Dual Federalism." *Virginia Law Review* 36, no. 1 (February 1950): 1–24.

Cust, Richard. *Charles I: A Political Life.* Harlow, UK: Pearson Longman, 2007.

Debevec, Robert M. "The Labor Injunction: Weapon or Tool." *Cleveland State Law Review* 4, no. 2 (1955): 102–13.

Dick, Diane Lourdes. "U.S. Tax Imperialism in Puerto Rico." *University Law Review* 65, no. 1 (2015): 1–86.

Elliott, Orrin Leslie. *The Tariff Controversy in the United States, 1789–1833.* Charleston, SC: Nabu Press, 2012.

Enos, Richard Leo, and Dean N. Constant. "A Bibliography of Ciceronian Rhetoric." *Rhetoric Society Quarterly* 6, no. 2 (1976): 21–28.

Goodwyn, Lawrence. *Democratic Promise: The Populist Moment in America.* New York: Oxford University Press, 1976.

Harrington, Fred H. "The Anti-imperialist Movement in the United States, 1898–1900." *Mississippi Valley Historical Review* 22, no. 2 (September 1935): 211–30.

Hartley, Lois. "Edgar Lee Masters, Political Essayist." *Journal of the Illinois State Historical Society (1908–1984)* 57, no. 3 (1964): 249–60.

Hicks, John D. *The Populist Revolt: A History of the Farmers' Alliance and the People's Party.* Lincoln: University of Nebraska Press, 1931.

Hofstadter, Richard. *The Age of Reform: From Bryan to F.D.R.* New York: Alfred A. Knopf, 1955.

Kazin, Michael. *A Godly Hero: The Life of William Jennings Bryan.* New York: Anchor Books, 2007.

Keresztes, Paul. "Nero, the Christians and the Jews in Tacitus and Clement of Rome." *Société d'Études Latines de Bruxelles* 43, no. 5 (1996): 404–413.

Kimmel, Michael. *Manhood in America: A Cultural History.* Oxford: Oxford University Press, 2018.

Kohn, Edward P. "A Benign Big Stick: Theodore Roosevelt and Global Policing." Review of *Theodore Roosevelt and World Order: Police Power in International Relations*, by James R. Holmes. *Journal of the Gilded Age and Progressive Era* 7, no. 1 (2008): 132–35.

Lears, Jackson. *Rebirth of a Nation: The Making of Modern America, 1877–1920*. New York: Harper Perennial, 2010.

Levillain, Charles-Edouard. "William III's Military and Political Career in Neo-Roman Context, 1672–1702." *Historical Journal* 48, no. 2 (2005): 321–50.

Linebaugh, Peter. *The Magna Carta Manifesto: Liberties and Commons for All*. Berkeley: University of California Press, 2009.

Mangan, J. A. and James Walvin, eds. *Manliness and Morality: Middle-Class Masculinity in Britain and America, 1800–1940*. Manchester, UK: Manchester University Press, 1987.

Meléndez, Edgardo. "Citizenship and the Alien Exclusion in the Insular Cases: Puerto Ricans in the Periphery of American Empire." *Centro Journal* 25, no. 1 (Spring 2013): 106–45.

McGerr, Michael. *A Fierce Discontent: The Rise and Fall of the Progressive Movement in America, 1870–1920*. Oxford: Oxford University Press, 2003.

Mitchell, Roger E., and Joyce P. Mitchell. "Schiller's William Tell: A Folkloristic Perspective." *Journal of American Folklore* 83, no. 327 (1970): 44–52.

Mombauer, Annika, and Wilhelm Deist, eds. *The Kaiser: New Research on Wilhelm II's Role in Imperial Germany*. Cambridge: Cambridge University Press, 2011.

Pérez, Louis A., Jr. "The Meaning of the *Maine*: Causation and the Historiography of the Spanish-American War." *Pacific Historical Review* 58, no. 3 (1989): 293–322.

Peterson, Brent O., and Martha B. Helfer. "Why Goethe Needs German Studies and Why German Studies Needs Goethe." *German Studies Review* 35, no. 3 (2012): 470–74.

Postel, Charles. *The Populist Vision*. New York: Oxford University Press, 2009.

Reese, Christine. "Controlling Print? Burton, Bastwick, and Prynne and the Politics of Memory." Ph.D. diss., Pennsylvania State University, 2007.

Russell, Herbert K. *Edgar Lee Masters: A Biography.* Urbana: University of Illinois Press, 2001.

Sage, Michael M. *The Republican Roman Army: A Sourcebook.* New York: Routledge, 2008.

Silbey, David J. *A War of Frontier and Empire: The Philippine-American War, 1899–1902.* New York: Hill and Wang, 2007.

Sklar, Martin J. *The Corporate Reconstruction of American Capitalism, 1890–1916: The Market, the Law, and Politics.* New York: Cambridge University Press, 1988.

Stacy, Jason. *Spoon River America: Edgar Lee Masters and the Myth of the American Small Town.* Urbana: University of Illinois Press, 2021.

Stevens, Michael E., and Steven B. Burg. *Editing Historical Documents: A Handbook of Practice.* Lanham, MD: AltaMira Press, 1997.

Thompson, James Westfall. "Edward Gibbon, 1737–1794." *Pacific Historical Review* 7, no. 2 (1938): 93–119.

Torruella, Juan R. "Ruling America's Colonies: The Insular Cases." *Yale Law and Policy Review* 32, no. 1 (2013): 57–95.

Werner, Shirley. "Vergilian Bibliography 2019–2020." *Vergilius* 66 (2020): 163–85.

Williams, Gordon. "Rudyard Kipling and His Critics." *Australian Quarterly* 8, no. 30 (1936): 65–70.

Yeats, A. W. "The Genesis of 'The Recessional.'" *University of Texas Studies in English* 31 (1952): 97–108.

INDEX

Edgar Lee Masters (1868-1950) was born in Garnett, Kansas and grew up in Petersburg and Lewiston, Illinois. As a young man, he studied law and relocated to Chicago in 1892. A lifelong Democrat, he stumped for Democratic Presidential Candidate William Jennings Bryan in 1896. Though a writer from youth, *Spoon River Anthology* (1915) proved to be his most successful work. Masters quit the law in 1923 to pursue writing full time, though none of his other works achieved the critical acclaim of *Spoon River Anthology*.